The Radiance Within

The Radiance Within

RECLAIM YOUR POWER, REWRITE YOUR STORY

CLARITZA RAUSCH PERALTA

THE PAPER HOUSE
PUBLISHING

Copyright © 2025 by Claritza Rausch Peralta

All rights reserved.

No part of this book may be reproduced in any form or by any electronic or mechanical means, including information storage and retrieval systems, without written permission from the author, except for the use of brief quotations in a book review.

Print in the USA

Published by The Paper House

www.thepaperhousebooks.com

Contents

Introduction   ix

PART ONE
THE FOUNDATION OF RADIANCE

1. Breaking Through the Darkness   3
2. Defining Your True Self   9
3. Cultivating Self-Awareness   15
4. Blossoming Through Faith and Action   22

PART TWO
EMBRACING RADIANCE

5. Reclaiming Your Power   33
6. Healing the Wounds   38
7. Self-Care as Empowerment   43
8. Developing Emotional Intelligence   50

PART THREE
CREATING YOUR DREAM LIFE

9. Visioning Your Way to Success   59
10. Goal Setting with Heart and Purpose   68
11. Overcoming Fear and Building Resilience   75
12. Manifestation in Action   80

PART FOUR
EMPOWERING OTHERS THROUGH RADIANCE

13. Breaking Free from Limiting Beliefs   89
14. The Power of Renewal   95
15. The Art of Leadership and Influence   101
16. Inspiring Others Through Your Story   104

17. Building Trust and Effective Communication   110
18. The Radiance Within   117

    PART FIVE
    NURTURING RADIANCE IN
    RELATIONSHIPS

19. Building Radiant Connections   127
20. Healing Relationships Through Forgiveness   130
21. Mindset and Personal Growth   134
22. Maintaining Your Radiance   137
23. Sharing Your Radiance   140

    Bonus Chapter: Navigating Life's Transitions   143
    Conclusion   147
    The Radiance Within: Chapter Notes   151

    About the Author   161

To everyone on the journey of self-discovery,
This book is for you—the courageous souls rediscovering their strength, the dreamers bravely rewriting their stories, and the hearts healing and rising anew. You are stronger, more radiant, and more capable than you can imagine. May you find light along your path, courage in every step, and peace in embracing the beauty that resides within you.

And to my beautiful angel in heaven, my grandmother, Mama Luisa—your love and strength inspire me every day. This book is infused with your warmth, and it is in your memory that I continue to grow and share my light with the world. Thank you for teaching me what true radiance means.

With all my love,
Claritza

Introduction

Imagine waking up every morning feeling energized, fully alive, knowing your purpose, and sensing the powerful radiance within you. What if, instead of succumbing to the world's expectations, you could live freely, embracing your unique gifts and shining your light unapologetically?

Welcome to the journey of **The Radiance Within**. This transformative path leads you back to your inner strength, enabling you to break free from the constraints that hold you back and step boldly into the life you were always meant to live. I believe that within each of us lies an extraordinary power—a source of light that may feel hidden beneath layers of doubt, fear, and past experiences. This light is not something we need to earn or prove; it is inherently ours, patiently waiting to be claimed.

In my memoir, **Blossoming into Radiance**, I opened my heart to share my profound journey from darkness to light—a

INTRODUCTION

journey marked by resilience, unwavering faith, and the essential practice of self-acceptance. However, as I continued to grow and evolve, I realized that radiance is not a final destination. It is a lifelong commitment to nurturing and honoring ourselves, one intentional choice at a time. Reclaiming our radiance means stepping into our power with both courage and purpose.

The Radiance Within is more than just a book; it is a roadmap guiding you back to your most authentic and vibrant self. Through a blend of personal stories, practical exercises, and transformative insights, we will explore how radiance can illuminate every facet of our lives—from our relationships and careers to our inner peace and overall well-being. Together, we will embark on a journey that includes:

- **Uncovering Purpose and Passion**: Identifying what ignites your spirit and infuses your life with meaning.
- **Reclaiming Power**: Learning to honor your unique strengths and face challenges gracefully and resiliently.
- **Living Authentically**: Embracing who you are—flaws and all—while shedding the limitations that hold you back.
- **Strengthening Connections**: Cultivating relationships that nourish and uplift your soul, creating a supportive community around you.

This book powerfully reminds us that radiance is not about

INTRODUCTION

achieving perfection but embracing wholeness. It's about recognizing the beauty within both the light and the shadows, understanding that every experience—joyful or painful—contributes to the magnificent person you are becoming.

Now is the time to take the first step toward reclaiming your power and rewriting your story. As you move through these pages, embrace the exercises, reflect deeply, and commit to making bold, intentional changes in your life.

My hope is that you will feel inspired and empowered to reclaim your light and embrace the life you truly deserve. Not someday, but starting right now. You have the power to rewrite your story, reclaim your narrative, and step into the brilliance that is uniquely yours. Every day is a new opportunity to cultivate your radiance and to live boldly, authentically, and unapologetically.

Welcome to your radiant journey. Embrace it fully and watch your life transform in ways you never thought possible. The time to shine is now!

PART ONE
The Foundation of Radiance

CHAPTER 1
Breaking Through the Darkness

"When you change the way you look at things, the things you look at change." — Wayne Dyer

The Journey of Resilience

As I sit in the quiet of my room, the weight of my past wraps around me like a familiar blanket. I can almost hear the echoes of my seven-year-old self, heart pounding in confusion, as I learned that the woman I had known as "Mom" was my grandmother. The moment felt surreal, as if the ground beneath my feet had shifted. The world I thought I understood crumbled in that instant, leaving me adrift in a sea of uncertainty. I was left grappling with feelings of loss, confusion, and rejection, unaware that this was merely the opening chapter of a complex narrative filled with unexpected revelations and hidden truths.

My life story has been a tapestry woven from threads of

struggle and discovery. Each twist and turn has molded me, revealing layers of strength I never knew existed. I think back to those early years—the nights spent lying awake, pondering my identity and place in a world that felt so foreign. Over time, I learned that resilience is not just about surviving but about blossoming, even in the harshest environments.

Unfolding Layers of Strength

With each passing year, the challenges I faced only multiplied. From turbulent relationships to battles with self-acceptance, every obstacle was a test of my spirit. Yet, within the turmoil, I discovered a wellspring of inner strength. I remember a pivotal moment when I found myself sitting on a park bench, tears streaming down my face after yet another heartbreak. I felt utterly defeated, but as I looked up at the sky, a small bird alighted on a nearby branch, singing its heart out. At that moment, I understood that life, like the bird, persists despite the storms.

My dear friend Sarah experienced her own awakening at a young age. Learning that her father was not who she believed him to be thrust her into a world of questions about her identity. But instead of allowing that revelation to shatter her, she transformed her pain into a driving force. Today, she is a counselor, guiding others through the labyrinth of family struggles. Her journey is a testament to the resilience that lies within us all.

As I invite you to walk alongside me on this path of self-discovery, I do so with the hope that my story resonates with yours. Together, we can peel back the layers of our experiences, embracing the beauty that lies within.

Navigating Uncertainty

There are moments in life when everything feels uncertain—when the future is clouded and the way forward seems obscured. I recall a time when I was engulfed in such uncertainty, navigating through the fog of despair. I felt like a ship lost at sea, buffeted by waves of doubt and fear. During those dark days, I learned the importance of self-reflection and the power of reaching out for support. The voices of friends and family were like lighthouses guiding me back to shore, illuminating paths I couldn't see on my own.

In **The Radiance Within**, I will share stories of heartache, triumph, despair, and hope. These narratives reveal the beauty in vulnerability and the strength that emerges from embracing our imperfections. We are not alone on this journey; by sharing our stories, we create a rich tapestry of shared human experience that binds us together.

As you delve into these pages, I invite you to pause and reflect on your own life:

- What challenges have shaped you?
- How have you found the courage to continue in the face of adversity?
- What insights have emerged from your own struggles?

These reflections are essential stepping stones to understanding who we are and who we are meant to become.

Embracing Vulnerability

Throughout my journey, I discovered an unexpected truth:

vulnerability is a source of strength. In a world that often equates strength with stoicism, I learned that true courage lies in allowing ourselves to be seen, raw, and real. I vividly remember the first time I opened my heart to someone I trusted. It felt like standing on the edge of a cliff, ready to leap into the unknown. The fear of judgment loomed large, but as I shared my truth, an overwhelming sense of relief washed over me.

Vulnerability is not about showcasing our flaws but embracing our shared humanity. It's accepting that we are all imperfect beings, navigating life's complexities together. Allowing ourselves to be vulnerable opens the door to genuine connection and healing.

The Power of Connection

When I embraced my vulnerability, it became a superpower, forging deeper connections with those around me. There's a profound beauty in sharing our joyful or painful experiences. Each moment of vulnerability became a bridge, linking me to others on a deeper level. I remember a heartwarming conversation with a stranger at a coffee shop who shared her own struggles with loss. In those shared moments of honesty, we both found solace, knowing we were not alone.

As I walked this path, I encountered individuals whose stories mirrored my own struggles and aspirations. Their experiences resonated within me, providing comfort and a sense of belonging. Each connection reminded me that our stories are intricately woven together, creating a rich tapestry of shared experiences.

Finding Purpose in Pain

In the darkest moments of my life, I often questioned the

purpose of my suffering. The pain felt relentless, a heavy burden that overshadowed everything else. I remember the day I lost my beloved mother, Mama Luisa. Her absence carved a profound void in my heart, a stark reminder of the fragility of life. Yet, even in my grief, I began to notice small glimmers of hope. Friends reached out with gentle words and acts of kindness, while strangers offered understanding nods that reminded me I was not alone.

Mama Luisa's wisdom and love continue to guide me, her teachings echoing in my mind. Amid my sorrow, I learned to channel my pain into action. I volunteered at local shelters, seeking to uplift others while honoring her legacy. Writing became my refuge, a way to articulate my grief and resilience. Each word penned was a step towards healing, a testament to the strength that was emerging from within me.

Though the journey is fraught with challenges, there is purpose in my pain. It has shaped me into a more compassionate and empathetic person, determined to impact the world positively. In those moments of darkness, I find comfort in knowing that Mama Luisa's light continues to shine through me, illuminating the path for others.

As I reflect on my experiences, I see that pain is not merely a source of suffering; it is a catalyst for growth. Though arduous, my journey is refining me like silver in a fire, revealing the beauty that lies within.

Reflection Questions

As you ponder my journey, consider these questions:

- How do my experiences resonate with your own?
- In what areas of your life have you struggled to embrace vulnerability, and how has that affected your relationships or personal growth?
- Can you recall a time when pain or struggle ultimately led to personal growth or insight? What lessons did you learn, and how have they shaped you?
- How can you utilize your own story to support or uplift someone else, and what actionable steps can you take to make that happen?

Let's turn the page and embark on this journey of growth and transformation together, with hearts open and spirits ready to soar.

CHAPTER 2
Defining Your True Self

"To be yourself in a world that is constantly trying to make you something else is the greatest accomplishment." — Ralph Waldo Emerson

Finding the courage to listen to my true self became one of the most challenging yet liberating journeys I would ever undertake. For years, I felt trapped in a whirlwind of external expectations, societal norms, and the constant nagging voices of doubt and fear echoing in my mind. It wasn't until I reached a breaking point—a moment of complete emotional exhaustion—that I realized I needed to redefine my inner voice. I had to transform the chaos around me into a clear, empowering melody that resonated with my soul.

I vividly remember one quiet evening, sitting in my bedroom, feeling the weight of the world pressing down on me. I felt like I was drowning in my own thoughts: "You're not good enough." "You'll never succeed." "What will others think?" Each whisper felt like a chain binding me to a version of myself that I no longer recognized. In that moment of despair, staring at the dim light from my bedside lamp, I picked up my journal, its pages worn and filled with fragments of my past thoughts and dreams, and began to write.

Journaling became my sanctuary—a sacred space where I could express my fears, hopes, and truths without fear of judgment. As I wrote, I uncovered layers of myself that had been buried under years of conditioning. I began to recognize that the voice inside me, often harsh and critical, was not my true self but a distorted echo of my fears, shaped by everything I had absorbed from the world around me.

Among those who have embarked on similar journeys, one inspiring example is Elizabeth Gilbert, author of "Eat, Pray, Love." After feeling lost in her marriage and career, Gilbert courageously decided to leave everything behind and travel the world searching for her true self. Through her journey, she confronted her fears, explored her passions, and ultimately discovered a voice that resonated with authenticity. Her story illustrates how the process of redefining one's inner voice can lead to profound personal transformation.

Another compelling case is that of J.K. Rowling, who faced numerous rejections before her Harry Potter series was published. Rowling struggled with self-doubt and depression but continued to write, driven by her passion for storytelling. Her unwavering commitment to her authentic voice and vision not only transformed her life but also impacted millions worldwide. Her journey reminds us that our true selves often emerge through perseverance and self-belief, even amidst adversity.

In addition to these well-known figures, many others from diverse backgrounds have shared their stories of self-discovery. For instance, Malala Yousafzai, a Pakistani activist for girls' education, faced life-threatening challenges for standing up for her beliefs. Her journey of resilience and advocacy reveals how listening to one's inner voice can ignite a powerful movement for change, inspiring countless others to find their own voices and stand up for their beliefs.

Similarly, consider the story of a young artist from a small town in Brazil who defied societal expectations by pursuing her passion for painting. Despite pressure to conform to conventional career paths, she dedicated herself to her art, using her work to express her experiences and cultural identity. Her journey illustrates that embracing one's true self can yield personal fulfillment and a rich contribution to the community and culture.

To aid in your own self-discovery, here are some actionable steps and exercises to help you peel back the layers of self-doubt and societal influence:

1. **Create a Personal Manifesto**: Write down your core values, beliefs, and what you stand for. This manifesto will serve as a guiding document that reflects your true self.

2. **Daily Reflection**: Set aside a few minutes each day to reflect on your feelings and actions. Ask yourself, "Did I honor my true self today?" and "What can I do tomorrow to stay aligned with my authentic self?"
3. **Practice Mindfulness**: Engage in mindfulness exercises to ground yourself in the present moment. This can help you become more aware of your thoughts and feelings, making it easier to identify your true desires.
4. **Seek Solitude**: Dedicate time to be alone without distractions. Use this quiet time to meditate or sit with your thoughts. This practice can help you connect with your inner voice more deeply.
5. **Connect with Nature**: Spend time outdoors, embracing the beauty around you. Nature can be a powerful catalyst for self-reflection and clarity.
6. **Engage in Creative Expression**: Try painting, drawing, or any form of art that allows you to express your feelings. Creativity can often reveal truths that words cannot.

Here are some journaling prompts to help you dive deeper into your self-discovery journey:

1. What are my deepest desires? Reflect on what truly ignites your passion. What dreams have you set aside because they seemed unrealistic or unworthy?

2. What fears do I need to confront? Acknowledge the fears holding you back. What limiting beliefs have you internalized, and how can you begin to dismantle them?
3. What does self-love mean to me? Consider how you can nurture yourself. What actions can you take to prioritize your well-being and happiness?
4. How do I want to show up in the world? Visualize the person you want to be. What qualities and values will guide you in embracing your authentic self?
5. What past experiences have shaped my self-perception? Identify key moments in your life that have influenced how you see yourself. How can you reframe these experiences to empower rather than limit you?
6. What brings me joy, and how can I incorporate more of it into my life? Take note of activities, people, or experiences that uplift you. How can you create space for more joy in your daily routine?

As you write, let your words be a declaration of your commitment to yourself. This letter is not just an exercise but a blueprint for your journey toward embracing your inner voice.

In redefining my inner voice, I discovered that listening to my true self was an act of bravery. It meant standing firm in my beliefs and desires, even when they contradicted what I had been taught. Each time I honored my voice over the noise of others, I reclaimed a piece of my power. I found strength in vulnerability, realizing that embracing my truth was the first step toward healing and transformation.

This chapter is just the beginning. As you continue on this journey, remember that the most profound changes often come from the whispers of your heart. Your inner voice is your greatest ally—nurture, listen, and allow it to guide you toward a life filled with authenticity and radiance.

Reflection Prompts:

- What three aspects of your life do you feel are not aligned with your true self?
- How can you begin to shift these aspects to reflect who you are better?

CHAPTER 3
Cultivating Self-Awareness

"Self-awareness is the ability to take an honest look at your life without any attachment to it being right or wrong." — Debbie Ford

As Debbie Ford suggests, honesty and examining our lives without the pressure of judgment are crucial for personal development. This honesty helps us uncover aspects of ourselves that may have been hidden under layers of defense mechanisms or societal norms. It requires bravery, as it may expose uncomfortable truths.

In this chapter, we will embark on a journey of self-discovery, highlighting the significance of self-awareness. Self-awareness involves recognizing and understanding our emotions, thoughts, and actions. It is more than just observing; it requires active engagement with our inner experiences. Developing self-awareness lays the groundwork for deep personal growth and meaningful change.

Mindfulness: Embracing the Present Moment

One of the most effective ways to cultivate self-awareness is through mindfulness. Mindfulness encourages us to immerse ourselves fully in the present moment, allowing us to observe our thoughts and feelings without judgment. This practice enables us to step back from immediate reactions and fosters a deeper understanding of our inner selves.

Mindfulness Exercise: Step-by-Step Guide

1. **Find a Quiet Space**: Choose a calm and comfortable spot where you won't be interrupted.
2. **Set a Timer**: Start with 5-10 minutes and increase the duration as you get more comfortable.
3. **Get Comfortable**: Sit in a chair or on the floor, maintaining a relaxed yet alert posture.
4. **Close Your Eyes**: Gently close your eyes to limit distractions.
5. **Focus on Your Breath**: Inhale deeply through your nose, letting your abdomen rise. Exhale slowly through your mouth, paying attention to your breathing rhythm.
6. **Acknowledge Thoughts**: When thoughts arise, recognize them without judgment. Observe each thought as a cloud in the sky, then let it drift away.
7. **Return to Your Breath**: If your mind wanders, gently bring your focus back to your breathing.

8. **Conclude the Session**: When your timer goes off, take a moment to notice how you feel before opening your eyes. Reflect on your experience.

Real-Life Example: Mindfulness in Action

Take Sarah, a busy corporate manager who often felt overwhelmed by her responsibilities. After learning about mindfulness, she set aside ten minutes each morning for deep breathing and meditation. Initially, quieting her mind was challenging, but over weeks, she noticed a significant improvement in her ability to manage stress. By practicing mindfulness, Sarah became more aware of her feelings, leading to better decision-making and improved relationships at work.

Introspection: A Journey Within

Introspection is another essential tool for enhancing self-awareness. It involves a deep examination of our thoughts, feelings, and experiences. Journaling can be particularly effective in this process. Set aside time each day to write about your thoughts and emotions.

Journaling Prompts for Introspection:

1. **Daily Reflection**: What emotions did I feel today? What triggered these feelings?
2. **Navigating Challenges**: How did I handle challenges today? What strategies worked or didn't work?

3. **Desires and Aspirations**: What do I truly desire? What steps can I take to align my life with these desires?
4. **Feedback Reflection**: What have I learned from recent feedback? How can I use this insight to improve my relationships?
5. **Gratitude Moments**: What am I thankful for today? How can gratitude shift my perspective?

Approach this process with patience and compassion. It may uncover uncomfortable truths, but these revelations can be powerful catalysts for growth. Embrace each insight as a step forward on your path of self-development.

Case Study: The Power of Journaling

Mark, a college student, struggled with anxiety and self-doubt. After a friend suggested journaling, he committed to writing down his thoughts each night. Initially, he focused on his worries. Over time, he began to highlight his achievements and aspirations. This shift helped Mark recognize negative thought patterns and replace them with affirmations of his strengths. Journaling became a crucial tool for self-reflection, allowing him to navigate his journey with confidence.

Understanding Emotions, Thoughts, and Actions

At the core of self-awareness is understanding the relationship between our emotions, thoughts, and behaviors. Our emotions often guide us, revealing what is truly important to us. By acknowledging our feelings, we can respond thoughtfully rather than react impulsively.

Our thought patterns also shape our perception of reality. By becoming aware of both positive and negative thoughts, we can challenge limiting beliefs and nurture a more optimistic mindset. Understanding how our thoughts and emotions interact empowers us to take control of our responses and actions.

As we enhance our self-awareness, we start to see that our behaviors often reflect our internal feelings. By understanding what motivates our actions, we can make choices that align with our values and aspirations.

Reflection Questions

- Which practices resonate with you on your journey toward self-awareness?
- Have you ever received feedback that changed your understanding of yourself?
- How could mindfulness enhance your daily life?

Additional Practical Exercises for Cultivating Self-Awareness:

1. **Body Scan Meditation**: Lie down comfortably, close your eyes, and focus on each body part, starting from your toes and moving upwards. Notice any sensations or areas of tension. This exercise connects physical sensations to emotions.
2. **Emotional Check-Ins**: Throughout the day, pause and ask yourself, "What am I feeling right now?" Identify the emotion and explore its triggers. This builds emotional awareness.
3. **Values Assessment**: List your core values (e.g., honesty, family, creativity). Reflect on how well your daily actions align with these values, clarifying your priorities and fostering intentional living.
4. **Visualization Exercise**: Imagine your ideal life or a goal you want to achieve. Picture every detail and note how it makes you feel. This can clarify your desires and motivate actions that align with your goals.
5. **Daily Affirmations**: Start each day by stating positive affirmations about yourself, such as "I am capable" or "I deserve love and respect." Affirmations can shift your mindset and reinforce self-belief.

Integrating these exercises into your routine can significantly enhance your journey toward self-awareness, making it practical and engaging. Embrace this process as a vital aspect of your personal growth.

CHAPTER 4
Blossoming Through Faith and Action

"Faith is taking the first step even when you don't see the whole staircase." — Martin Luther King Jr.

As I embarked on my journey of self-discovery and personal growth, one crucial element emerged as my guiding light—faith. This was not merely a passive belief in a higher power; it was a dynamic force propelling me forward, especially during uncertain times. Faith intertwined with my spirituality, intuition, and a deep belief in a purpose greater than myself.

The Role of Faith in My Journey

In those moments when I felt utterly lost, faith became my anchor. I vividly remember a particularly tough period when self-doubt loomed over me like a heavy cloud, obscuring my vision and dimming my spirit. During these challenging times, I turned to my faith—praying for clarity and direction. It was in these quiet moments of surrender that I uncovered a profound truth: faith isn't about having all the answers; it's about trusting the journey, even when the path ahead seems unclear.

Listening to my intuition also played a vital role. I learned to pay attention to that subtle inner voice—the one that encouraged me to take risks when fear tried to hold me back. This blend of faith and intuition guided my steps, helping me navigate life's complexities with a sense of purpose.

The Dance of Faith and Action

One of the most important lessons I learned was how to balance faith with action. One of the most significant lessons I learned was the importance of balancing faith with action. Let me share how Radiant Dreams Co. came to life. After the loss of my grandmother, I found myself working two jobs, often clocking in over 16 hours a day, trying to distract myself from the grief.

One evening, after an especially exhausting day, I collapsed onto my couch and recognized that I needed to make a change.

With my eyes closed, I envisioned creating a community dedicated to supporting women across the globe who felt trapped and uncertain. Although the excitement surged within me, doubts quickly followed: How could I embark on this journey without the necessary resources or funding?

That night, I made a decision to take a leap of faith. I penned my idea for Radiant Dreams Co., a vibrant space for sharing diverse experiences. It felt audacious, yet as I began to engage with others on social media, a mix of excitement and fear coursed through me.

In the weeks that followed, I devoted countless hours to

nurturing this dream—networking, refining my vision, and seeking support. One evening, I received my first message from a woman who had found our community. She shared how desperately she needed a space like this and how she felt truly seen for the first time in years. In that moment, I understood the profound impact of faith coupled with action.

Our initiative blossomed, forging connections in ways I had never anticipated. It served as a powerful reminder that faith isn't just about waiting for opportunities; it's about taking initiative and stepping beyond our comfort zones. That leap of faith transformed my life and empowered countless women to discover their voices within our community.

Many believe that trusting the process means passively waiting for opportunities to arise. However, I learned that faith is an active force that compels us to make bold moves.

Consider this: faith without action can lead to stagnation, while action taken without faith can lead to exhaustion and burnout. The real magic occurs when we harmonize both—when we act inspired by our beliefs.

Throughout my journey, I often pondered: What does it mean to move forward while maintaining faith? I realized it involves setting clear intentions and taking steps that resonate with my core beliefs. Every action, no matter how small, plays a crucial role in bringing my dreams to fruition.

Many people think that trusting the process means waiting passively for opportunities to come to them. However, I discovered that faith is an active force that requires us to take bold steps forward.

Turning Dreams into Plans

To help you blend faith and decisive action in your life, here are some actionable steps to implement right away:

1. **Set Intentions with Clarity**: Begin by defining what you want to achieve. Write down your dreams and aspirations with specific details. Instead of saying, "I want to be happy," articulate what happiness means for you: "I want to cultivate joy by spending quality time with loved ones, pursuing my passions, and practicing gratitude every day."
2. **Embrace Daily Affirmations**: Create a list of affirmations that resonate with your intentions. Repeat these affirmations daily to reinforce your belief in your ability to achieve your dreams. For example, say, "I trust my journey and embrace the steps I need to take to fulfill my dreams."
3. **Take Inspired Action**: Identify small, actionable steps you can take daily or weekly that align with your intentions. This might include networking, enrolling in a course, or starting a new project. Ensure these actions feel inspired rather than forced.
4. **Cultivate a Faith Practice**: Incorporate spiritual practices into your daily routine, whether through prayer, meditation, or mindfulness. These practices will help you connect with your higher self and foster a sense of trust in the process.

5. **Reflect and Adjust**: Make time to reflect on your journey. Are your actions aligning with your intentions? What has worked, and what hasn't? This reflection will allow you to adjust your plans while maintaining faith in your direction.
6. **Celebrate Small Wins**: Acknowledge and celebrate every step you take toward your goals, no matter how minor. Recognizing these victories reinforces your faith in yourself and the process.
7. **Stay Open to Possibilities**: Be receptive to the unexpected. Sometimes, faith leads us in directions we didn't foresee. Embrace these detours, knowing they may present opportunities that align with your higher purpose.

By following these steps, you will create a powerful synergy between faith and action. As you embrace your potential, you will find that your dreams are not just distant fantasies but tangible possibilities waiting to be realized.

The Blossoming Process

Faith and action are not separate; they are intertwined in a dance that propels us toward our dreams. By embracing faith while taking decisive action, we can navigate life's uncertainties with confidence and grace.

Let's remember that blossoming into our fullest selves is a continual process—a beautiful unfolding that requires patience, perseverance, and the courage to trust in ourselves and the path ahead.

In moments when doubt creeps in, let us lean on our faith to illuminate the way forward. Trust that each small action, fueled by belief, is a brushstroke painting the masterpiece of our lives. We are artists of our destiny, shaping a future that reflects our deepest desires and truest selves.

Inspiring Examples

Many people in history have shown how faith can influence their actions and create positive change. In this piece, we will look at the lives of two incredible women and one inspiring man who have lived out their faith and made a significant difference in the world.

Oprah Winfrey: The Champion of Dreams

Oprah Winfrey, often celebrated as a champion of dreams, has inspired millions through her remarkable journey and unwavering belief in the power of possibility. Known for her groundbreaking career in media and philanthropy, Oprah encourages individuals to dream big and pursue their passions with courage and authenticity. Her teachings are deeply rooted in self-discovery and personal empowerment, emphasizing the importance of aligning one's actions with a higher purpose.

Oprah's journey is a testament to resilience as she overcame numerous personal struggles, including challenges in her early life. She attributes her success to her strong belief in her own potential and the transformative power of connection and compassion. By sharing her experiences and insights, Oprah empowers others to break free from limitations and embrace their true selves. Her commitment to uplifting others is evident in her efforts to inspire and support individuals in manifesting their dreams and living fulfilling purpose-driven lives.

Joyce Meyer: A Catalyst for Change

Joyce Meyer, a renowned Christian author and speaker, has dedicated her life to spreading messages of hope, healing, and empowerment. Her ministry, Joyce Meyer Ministries, reaches millions worldwide, offering practical advice and spiritual guidance to those seeking transformation. Joyce's faith journey is a testament to resilience and unwavering trust in God's plan.

Having faced numerous personal challenges, including abuse and adversity, Joyce found strength in her faith. She used her experiences to connect with others, encouraging them to embrace vulnerability as a path to healing. Her teachings emphasize the importance of trust, forgiveness, and living authentically. Joyce's faith in action shines through her dedication to helping others overcome their struggles and find peace through spiritual growth.

Steve Harvey: Faith as a Foundation for Success

Steve Harvey, a celebrated comedian, author, and television host, has often spoken about the pivotal role faith has played in his life and career. Steve's journey to success was far from easy; he faced numerous setbacks and hardships. However, his faith remained a constant source of strength and inspiration, guiding him through life's challenges.

Steve Harvey openly shares how his faith in God has shaped his perspective, decisions, and achievements. He believes that faith, combined with hard work and perseverance, can lead to extraordinary outcomes. Through his humor and storytelling, Steve encourages others to trust in their unique paths and embrace the power of faith in action. His life serves as a testament to the transformative impact of believing in something greater than oneself.

Living Out Faith Through Action

These inspiring individuals demonstrate that faith is not just a belief but a dynamic force that can drive meaningful change. Whether through motivating others, offering spiritual guidance, or sharing personal journeys, their actions reflect the profound impact of living with faith.

As we continue our own journeys, let us draw inspiration from these examples and recognize the power of faith to shape our lives, guiding us toward a radiant future filled with purpose, hope, and empowerment.

Reflection Prompts:

- In what areas of your life do you need to exercise more faith?
- How can you take inspired action that aligns with your beliefs and aspirations?
- What small steps can you take today to reinforce your faith in the journey ahead?

PART TWO
Embracing Radiance

CHAPTER 5
Reclaiming Your Power

"Your life does not get better by chance, it gets better by change."
— Jim Rohn

There comes a moment in every person's life—a pivotal juncture—where you must confront the uncomfortable truth: you've been living for others rather than for yourself. This realization can feel like a thunderclap, shaking the very foundations of your existence. I vividly remember the day I chose to love myself enough to walk away from relationships and situations that no longer served me. It was not an easy decision, nor was it made in a vacuum. It was born from a blend of desperation and a flicker of hope that life could be different.

For years, I found myself bending over backward to please others, often at the expense of my own happiness. I was the friend everyone turned to, the one who sacrificed her own needs for the sake of others. I wore this role like a badge of honor, convincing myself that my worth was directly tied to my ability to care for those around me. But deep down, I felt hollow and exhausted, constantly running on fumes. The vibrant colors of my life faded into a dull gray as I poured all my energy into maintaining the happiness of others while neglecting my own.

The pivotal moment came when I found myself in a situation that felt unbearable. I was caught in a toxic situationship—one that drained my energy and self-esteem like a leaky bucket. I felt suffocated by the weight of their expectations and the fear of disappointing them. There was a nagging voice inside me saying, "You deserve better than this." Yet, fear held me captive, whispering that I would be alone if I chose to walk away. It was a battle between my longing for freedom and the chains of insecurity that kept me tethered to a life that no longer sparked joy.

It took countless sleepless nights and tearful reflections for me to finally recognize that reclaiming my power meant risking the comfort of the familiar. I had to shut down my social media, disconnect from the noise, and focus solely on what I wanted and needed. In that silence, I faced my fears head-on. I asked myself hard questions: What do I truly want? Who am I without these external validations? Each question was like peeling back layers of an onion, revealing the raw, vulnerable core of my true self.

In those quiet moments, I began to rediscover myself—my passions, my dreams, and the values that truly mattered to me. I remember sitting alone in my room, journaling late into the night, pouring out my heart, and letting the ink on the page be my confessor. I wrote about the anger I felt towards myself for allowing others to dictate my happiness, the guilt I carried for wanting to prioritize my needs, and the overwhelming relief I felt when I finally made the decision to choose myself. That act of writing became a cathartic release, a way to unearth the emotions I had buried for so long.

Reclaiming my power meant setting boundaries that felt uncomfortable at first. I started saying "no" to things that drained me. I recall a particular afternoon when I had to confront the guy I had been seeing for years, who had only been using me for pleasure. My instinct screamed, "Say no!" but I hesitated, fearing his reaction. At that moment, I took a deep breath and firmly said, "I'm sorry, but I can't continue this anymore." I felt a rush of adrenaline, a mix of fear and exhilaration. It was a small victory, but it marked the beginning of a new chapter in my life. Each "no" became a declaration of my self-worth, a reminder that I mattered. I learned to trust my instincts, to listen to that inner voice that had been silenced for so long.

Each time I chose myself, I felt a little more whole, a little more radiant, as if I was slowly piecing together a jigsaw puzzle that had been scattered for years. I want you to know that self-love is the root of all transformation. Without it, no amount of external success can fulfill you. It's a lesson I had to learn the hard way. I'm still a work in progress, but each day, I am more aware of my worth. I encourage you to reflect on your own life: What relationships or habits are you holding onto that no longer serve you? What would it feel like to choose yourself, to reclaim your power?

Take a moment to envision what your life would look like if you embraced self-love wholeheartedly. Picture yourself setting boundaries, saying no when necessary, and recognizing your worth. Can you see how liberating it would be to prioritize your own happiness? I challenge you to take the first step toward this journey. Write down what it means for you to reclaim your power and how you plan to honor yourself moving forward.

Reclaiming your power is a journey, not a destination. There will be days when you stumble, but that's okay. Each step you take is a testament to your growth and a celebration of the beautiful, radiant person you are becoming. Embrace the journey, and know that every moment spent investing in yourself is a moment well spent. You are worth it.

Checklist for Identifying and Enforcing Personal Boundaries:

1. **Reflect on Relationships**: List people or situations draining your energy and note their impact on your well-being.
2. **Identify Boundaries**: Define specific boundaries for each relationship to protect your energy.
3. **Practice Saying No**: Choose a boundary to enforce this week and plan your response.
4. **Recognize Worth**: List five qualities or achievements that affirm your self-worth and reflect on their significance.

5. **Visualize Self-Love**: Imagine a day prioritizing your needs, confidently setting boundaries, and note your feelings and actions to achieve it.
6. **Create an Affirmation**: Write a personal affirmation reinforcing your worth and repeat it daily.
7. **Track Progress**: Journal your experiences implementing boundaries and affirmations, noting feelings and changes in self-perception.

As you engage in this exercise, remember: you are worthy of love and respect, starting with yourself. Embrace this truth and let it guide you on your journey to reclaiming power and self-worth. Every effort you make counts!

CHAPTER 6
Healing the Wounds

"You cannot heal what you do not reveal." — Joyce Meyer

Anyone who knows me can see how deeply my grandmother influenced my life. She was more than just the mother who cared for me after my own mother left when I was just nine months old. She was my foundation, my source of hope, and the person I loved most in the world. Losing her felt like a part of me was ripped away. The pain of her absence wrapped around me like a heavy blanket, leaving me feeling cold and overwhelmed.

In the days after her passing, I was in shock, unable to grasp the reality of my loss. I moved through life in a fog, each moment feeling unreal. It was as if I was living in a different world—a world where my grandmother was no longer there, and her laughter was just a faint memory. I felt lost and consumed by a deep emptiness. The person who had taught me about love, resilience, and strength was gone, and I struggled to find my way in a world without her.

The grief was overwhelming. Even the simplest tasks felt monumental. I would sit in silence, tears streaming down my face, longing for just one more hug or conversation. The pain felt all-consuming, and I often wondered how I could ever heal from this deep wound.

Amid my sorrow, I noticed my son, Liam. He looked at me with worry in his eyes, reflecting the confusion he felt. I realized that my sadness was not only my burden; it was affecting him, too. It broke my heart to see how my grief overshadowed the joy he needed in his life. I knew I had to change things—not just for my sake but for his as well.

In my darkest moments, I turned to God, praying for strength. I asked for guidance to help me through this painful chapter. In those moments of desperation, I felt a gentle reassurance reminding me that healing is a journey, not a destination.

As the days turned into weeks, I learned that grief is not a straight path but rather a winding road filled with ups and downs. In my sorrow, I began to find small sparks of hope. I understood that my grandmother wouldn't want me to stay in despair; she would want me to honor her by embracing life.

I started to face my pain, allowing myself to feel it instead of pushing it away. I took up journaling, writing letters to her, and sharing memories that made me smile. With each word, I felt a little of my grief lift. This process showed me that healing isn't a straight line; it's about revisiting pain with new strength.

Over time, I realized that my grandmother's spirit lived on in me. Her strength became my strength. I reflected on her teachings—perseverance, kindness, and believing in the beauty of life. I made a choice to honor her by living authentically and chasing my dreams with the same passion she had shown me.

This experience taught me that healing isn't about forgetting; it's about turning pain into purpose. I found strength in being vulnerable, recognizing that it's okay to grieve while also embracing the joy she brought into my life. Each time I smiled or pursued my dreams, I was honoring her memory and legacy.

As I began to heal, I focused on being a better mother to Liam. I wanted him to see that even in pain, life can hold beauty and hope. I started sharing stories about his great-grandmother and the love she had for him. I wanted him to understand that while grief is part of life, so is joy. I learned that it's possible to hold both feelings at once—to grieve for my loss while celebrating the love that surrounds us.

Grief, I realized, is a universal experience that takes many forms. It can come from losing a friend who was once a cornerstone of your life or from the end of a cherished job that shaped your identity. It could even stem from the loss of a dream that you held dear but has since faded away. Each of these experiences carries its own weight and complexity, yet they all connect us in shared understanding. Just as I navigate my sorrow for my grandmother, others are finding their way through their own losses, discovering that in the midst of heartache, there is still room for hope and connection.

I encourage you to reflect on your own wounds—those

moments that weigh heavily on your heart. Healing takes time and compassion. It's okay to feel your pain but remember that it can also lead to growth. As you confront your struggles, ask yourself: What can I learn from my experiences? How can I turn my pain into strength?

Guided Self-Reflection Exercise: Confronting an Old Wound

1. **Find a Quiet Space**: Choose a comfortable and quiet place where you won't be disturbed. Settle in, take a few deep breaths, and allow yourself to relax.
2. **Identify the Wound**: Think about an old emotional wound that still affects you today. It could be a past relationship, a loss, or a moment of betrayal. Acknowledge its presence in your life without judgment.
3. **Visualize the Experience**: Close your eyes and visualize the moment associated with this wound. Try to recall the details: what happened, how you felt, and the emotions that arose. Allow yourself to fully experience these feelings, but keep a sense of safety in mind.
4. **Write It Down**: Take a notebook or journal and write about the experience. Describe the event, your emotions at the time, and how it has impacted you. Be honest and thorough; this is for your eyes only.
5. **Reflect on the Lessons**: After writing, take a moment to reflect on what this experience has taught

you. Consider how it has shaped your beliefs, behaviors, and relationships. What insights can you draw from it?

6. **Forgiveness and Release**: If you feel ready, consider extending forgiveness to yourself or others involved. This doesn't mean excusing the behavior but rather freeing yourself from the burden of carrying this hurt. Write a letter of forgiveness, whether you choose to send it or keep it for yourself.

7. **Set an Intention for Healing**: Close your exercise by setting a positive intention for your healing journey. This could be a simple affirmation, such as "I am worthy of healing" or "I release this pain and embrace my growth."

8. **Conclude with Self-Care**: End the session by engaging in a self-care activity that nurtures you—whether it's a warm bath, a walk in nature, or some quiet meditation. Acknowledge the courage it took to confront this wound and honor yourself for taking this important step toward healing.

Remember, healing is a journey, and it's okay to take your time. As you navigate through your grief, keep in mind that healing is not a linear process. There will be moments of joy that gradually return as you honor your journey. Just as the seasons change, so too will your experiences and emotions. Allow yourself the grace to feel each part of your journey, knowing that brighter days are ahead and that you are not alone in your healing.

CHAPTER 7
Self-Care as Empowerment

"Self-care is giving the world the best of you, instead of what's left of you." — Katie Reed

Self-care is often misunderstood as a luxury or indulgence, but I have come to see it as an essential necessity for anyone looking to cultivate a vibrant life. It goes beyond pampering ourselves with bubble baths or occasional treats; it involves honoring our mind, body, and spirit through intentional practices that nourish our well-being.

Throughout my journey of embracing my inner radiance, I faced numerous challenges that threatened to dim my light. I realized that to truly flourish, I first needed to take responsibility for my own self-care. This realization was crucial. I learned that when we neglect ourselves, we cannot fully show up for others or pursue our dreams. It became evident that self-care is a powerful expression of self-love, and through this love, we reclaim our strength.

At one point, the chaos in my life became overwhelming, leading me to take a significant step: I decided to deactivate my social media accounts. The constant flow of curated images and highlight reels fueled my insecurities and self-doubt. I found myself questioning my worth and my journey. Unplugging was not just a break; it was a powerful affirmation that I was prioritizing my mental and emotional health above everything else.

In this newfound space, I began exploring various self-care practices that could support my healing and growth. I started with meditation, seeking moments of stillness to reconnect with my true self. Initially, it was difficult to quiet my mind, but with practice, I discovered peace and clarity in those moments. Each session became a refuge where I could release the day's burdens and invite the light of self-acceptance.

Physical movement also became a cornerstone of my self-care routine. I realized that moving my body—whether through yoga, dancing, or simply walking—was a way to release pent-up emotions and energize my spirit. I began to see exercise not just as a means to physical fitness but as a celebration of what my body can do and a way to honor my strength and resilience.

Nutrition played a vital role as well. I shifted my focus from restrictive diets to nourishing my body with wholesome foods. I came to view meals as a form of self-care—each ingredient chosen with love, each bite an affirmation of my commitment to my well-being. Cooking turned into a creative outlet, and I found joy in experimenting with flavors and textures, deeply connecting with the food I consumed.

Alongside these practices, I embraced mindfulness as a daily habit. I made it a point to write down three things I was grateful for every evening. This simple act shifted my perspective, allowing me to focus on abundance instead of lack. It helped me cultivate a mindset rooted in positivity, making me more aware of the blessings in my life.

As I dedicated myself to my self-care journey, I noticed the transformation not only in my life but also in the lives of those around me. When we nurture ourselves, we become a source of inspiration and empowerment for others. My relationships deepened, and I began attracting people who mirrored the love and light I was nurturing within.

30-Day Self-Care Challenge

To help you embrace the transformative power of self-care, I invite you to take on a 30-day self-care challenge. This challenge focuses on nurturing mindfulness, nutrition, rest, and joy, providing a structured path to enhance your well-being:

Week 1: Mindfulness

- Day 1: Start a daily meditation or prayer practice, aiming for at least 5 to 10 minutes each day.
- Day 2: Take a mindful walk, paying attention to your surroundings.
- Day 3: Write a gratitude list of at least five things you appreciate.
- Day 4: Spend 15 minutes journaling about your feelings.
- Day 5: Practice deep breathing exercises for relaxation.
- Day 6: Enjoy a quiet moment with a cup of tea, reflecting on your day.
- Day 7: Engage in mindful eating, savoring each bite.

Week 2: Nutrition

- Day 8: Plan and prepare a healthy meal for the week.
- Day 9: Try a new fruit or vegetable.
- Day 10: Drink at least 8 glasses of water today.
- Day 11: Replace a processed snack with a healthier option.
- Day 12: Cook a meal mindfully, enjoying each step of the process.
- Day 13: Share a healthy recipe with a friend.
- Day 14: Reflect on how different foods make you feel.

Week 3: Rest

- Day 15: Create a relaxing bedtime routine and go to bed early.
- Day 16: Dedicate a day to rest—no work or obligations.
- Day 17: Take a short nap when you feel tired.
- Day 18: Spend time doing nothing—allow your mind to wander.
- Day 19: Read an inspiring book.
- Day 20: Journal about the importance of rest in your life.
- Day 21: Enjoy a relaxing bath or engage in a self-care ritual.

Final Days: Reflection and Integration

- Day 22: Engage in a hobby that brings you joy.
- Day 23: Spend time with loved ones doing something fun.
- Day 24: Watch a movie or read a book that makes you laugh.
- Day 25: Create a vision board for your dreams and goals.
- Day 26: Write a letter to yourself celebrating your achievements.
- Day 27: Dance like no one's watching!

- Day 28: Plan a day trip or outing to explore something new.
- Day 29: Reflect on your self-care journey over the past month.
- Day 30: Set intentions for continuing your self-care practice moving forward.

Embracing the Power of Self-Care

As you embark on this self-care challenge, remember that self-care is not a selfish act; it is a declaration of your worthiness. By prioritizing self-care, you equip yourself with the tools to face life's challenges with resilience and grace.

When we care for ourselves, we become more capable of supporting others and contributing positively to the world around us. Embrace this power and let self-care illuminate your path toward a more radiant and fulfilling life.

Reflective Questions:

1. How do you currently define self-care in your life, and what practices do you prioritize?
2. What challenges have you faced in your self-care journey, and how have they impacted your well-being?
3. In what ways have you noticed a change in your relationships and interactions with others as a result of prioritizing self-care?

4. What specific self-care practices resonate most with you, and how can you integrate them into your daily routine?
5. How does your understanding of self-care shift when you view it as an expression of self-love rather than a luxury?
6. What emotions or thoughts arise when you consider taking a break from social media or other external distractions?
7. How does mindfulness play a role in your self-care, and what techniques do you find most effective for cultivating it?
8. In what ways can you celebrate your progress throughout your self-care challenge, even the small victories?
9. How can you ensure that your self-care practices remain sustainable and not just a temporary focus during the challenge?
10. What intentions will you set for yourself as you continue your self-care journey beyond the 30-day challenge?

CHAPTER 8
Developing Emotional Intelligence

"When awareness is brought to an emotion, power is brought to your life." — Tara Meyer Robson

Professionally, I work in a bank and have been doing so for over ten years. One typical Monday morning, I was tucked behind my desk, reviewing the day's appointments, when a visibly distressed customer approached the counter. Her face was flushed, and her hands trembled as she clutched a bank statement.

"Excuse me, I need help," she stammered, her voice barely above a whisper. I could see the fear in her eyes, and something in my gut told me this was more than just a routine banking issue.

I stepped out from behind the counter and invited her to sit down. "Of course, I'm here to help. What seems to be the problem?" I asked, keeping my tone warm and inviting. As she settled into the chair, I noticed the way her fingers fidgeted with the edge of the statement.

"It's my account. There's a charge here that doesn't make sense," she said, her voice breaking. "I think I'm being robbed."

At that moment, I felt a surge of empathy. I could imagine the fear of losing money and the anxiety of feeling vulnerable. Instead of diving straight into the numbers, I took a deep breath and focused on her emotions. "I can only imagine how stressful this must be for you," I said, maintaining eye contact to show her she wasn't alone in this moment.

As she recounted her concerns, I practiced self-regulation, reminding myself to stay calm and composed. It would have been easy to feel overwhelmed by her distress, but I was determined to create a safe space for her to express her feelings. I nodded along, validating her emotions. "It's completely understandable to feel this way," I reassured her. "Let's take a look together and see what's going on."

We examined her account step by step, and as I clicked through the transactions, I could see the tension slowly begin to ease on her shoulders. Finally, I located the charge she was worried about. It turned out to be an automatic payment she had forgotten about—one she had set up months prior.

"Here it is," I said gently. "This is a subscription fee that you may have signed up for without realizing it," I explained the charge, keeping my voice steady and calm. "Would you like me to help you cancel it?"

Relief washed over her face as she nodded, tears of frustration turning into a smile of gratitude. "Thank you so much. I was so scared; I didn't know what to do."

"It's my pleasure," I replied, feeling warmth spread through me. "I'm glad we could sort this out together."

As she left the bank, I reflected on how emotional intelligence had played a pivotal role in that interaction. Empathy allowed me to connect with her on a human level, while self-regulation helped me maintain my composure and offer the support she needed. It was a reminder that in the world of banking, numbers, and transactions are important, but the emotions of those we serve are just as crucial.

In the days that followed, I carried that experience with me, recognizing that emotional intelligence was not just a skill to develop but a vital part of creating meaningful connections in both my personal and professional life.

Emotional intelligence (EI) is essential in our daily interactions. It involves understanding and managing our emotions while being aware of the feelings of others. This chapter simplifies emotional intelligence into three key components: self-regulation, empathy, and social skills. It also offers practical tips for enhancing these abilities to foster better relationships.

What is Emotional Intelligence?

Emotional intelligence refers to the ability to recognize, understand, and manage our emotions and those of others. The three main aspects are:

1. Self-Regulation: This involves controlling your emotions and impulses. It means being aware of your

feelings and managing them so you can respond thoughtfully rather than react impulsively.
2. Empathy: Empathy is about understanding and sharing the feelings of others. It goes beyond sympathy; it requires putting yourself in someone else's shoes and seeing things from their perspective.
3. Social Skills: These are the abilities that help us communicate and interact effectively with others. Strong social skills enable us to build relationships, resolve conflicts, and connect with people on a deeper level.

How to Improve Emotional Intelligence

Enhancing your emotional intelligence requires commitment and practice. Here are some straightforward strategies:

1. Cultivating Self-Regulation

- Mindfulness Practices: Engage in activities like meditation or deep breathing to better recognize and manage your emotions.
- Journaling: Write about your feelings and reactions to various situations. This helps identify patterns and areas for improvement.
- Pause Before Responding: When faced with upsetting situations, take a moment to think before reacting. This pause can lead to clearer responses.

2. Developing Empathy

- Active Listening: Fully concentrate on the person speaking. Show that you value their feelings and respond in a way that acknowledges their perspective.
- Perspective-Taking: Consider how others might feel in specific situations. Ask yourself what they are experiencing.
- Volunteer: Participate in community service to learn about different experiences, which can enhance your understanding of others.

3. Strengthening Social Skills

- Effective Communication: Practice expressing your thoughts and feelings clearly and kindly. Use "I" statements to avoid blaming others.
- Conflict Resolution: View conflicts as opportunities for growth. Focus on finding solutions instead of assigning blame.
- Networking: Seek opportunities to meet new people. Building connections can improve your social skills.

The Ripple Effect of Emotional Intelligence

As you improve your emotional intelligence, you may notice positive changes in your relationships. Better self-regulation can reduce stress, empathy can strengthen connections, and strong social skills can enhance teamwork and collaboration.

In conclusion, emotional intelligence is a skill that can be developed over time. By working on your EI, you can improve your life and positively influence those around you.

Questions for You:

1. What emotions do you find challenging to manage?
2. How can you incorporate empathy into your daily interactions?
3. Reflect on a recent conflict—how might better emotional intelligence have changed the outcome?

PART THREE

Creating Your Dream Life

CHAPTER 9

Visioning Your Way to Success

"The only thing worse than being blind is having sight but no vision." — Helen Keller

Throughout my personal growth journey, I have learned an essential truth: visualization is a powerful method for connecting our dreams with reality. It has transformed my life, enabling me to cultivate a meaningful and joyful existence. Visualization aligns with the idea expressed in Habakkuk 2:2, which emphasizes clarity in our goals and dreams: "Write the vision and make it plain." By articulating our aspirations, we create a roadmap leading us toward the future we desire.

The Transformative Power of Visualization

Visualization is not mere daydreaming; it is a potent tool for manifesting our dreams. One of my greatest inspirations in this area is Terri Savelle Foy, whose passion for dreams is infectious.

Her energy ignites excitement about pursuing our goals. When she speaks about visualization, it feels like a motivational rally, urging us to chase our dreams. Terri's uplifting messages inspire those around her to aim for their best selves.

She teaches us to visualize our goals as if they are already achieved. By vividly imagining the life we want and embracing the emotions associated with those dreams, we strengthen our belief in their possibility. Picture Terri on a mountaintop, enthusiastically cheering with confetti falling around her—that's the kind of energy visualization can evoke!

As I practiced visualization, I found it to be a bridge between my present circumstances and the life I longed for. It freed me from societal expectations and helped me focus on what truly mattered to me. Moreover, visualization is a journey of self-discovery. It prompts us to reflect on our true desires and the possibilities we can achieve. So, take a moment to close your eyes and imagine your dream life. What does it look like? How does it feel? Allow yourself to dream boldly and without limits. Remember, just beyond your comfort zone lies the life you've always wanted.

Visualization Tips for Better Results

To enhance your visualization practice, consider these tips:

1. Be Specific: Focus on specific details. Instead of picturing a generic dream home, imagine the color of the walls, the layout of the rooms, and the feelings you'll experience living there.

2. Use All Your Senses: Engage your senses. Imagine the sounds, smells, and textures associated with your goals. This multi-sensory approach makes the experience more vivid and impactful.
3. Create a Routine: Set aside dedicated time daily for visualization. Consistency helps reinforce your vision and keeps your goals at the forefront of your mind.
4. Visualize with Emotion: Connect emotionally with your visualizations. Feel the excitement, joy, and fulfillment as if you've already achieved your goals. Emotions are powerful motivators.
5. Incorporate Movement: Try incorporating physical movement, like walking or stretching, as you visualize. This can enhance your energy and help you embody the feelings associated with your aspirations.
6. Keep a Visualization Journal: Document your visualization experiences and the emotions you feel. This practice can help track your progress and refine your goals.
7. Practice Gratitude: After each visualization session, express gratitude for what you have and what you're working toward. Gratitude shifts your mindset and attracts more positive outcomes.

Creating Your Vision Board

One of the most impactful methods for practicing visualization is by making a vision board—a concrete representation of your goals. If you're unfamiliar with what a vision board is, it's a collage of images, words, and phrases that embody your aspirations and dreams. This visual tool acts as a reminder of what you wish to accomplish, enabling you to concentrate on your intentions and bring your desires to life. Here's a guide to creating a vision board that truly resonates with your highest self:

1. Gather Your Materials: Collect a poster board or corkboard, scissors, glue, magazines, printouts, and any other inspiring materials that resonate with you.
2. Set Your Intentions: Reflect on what you genuinely want to manifest across various life areas—career, relationships, health, and personal growth. Writing these intentions down clarifies your vision and reinforces your commitment.
3. Collect Images and Words: Seek out images, quotes, and words that resonate with your aspirations. Cut them from magazines or print them online. Choose visuals that evoke strong emotions and inspiration, serving as reminders of your potential.
4. Arrange Your Board: Start placing the images and words on your board. Trust your instincts—there's no right or wrong way to arrange them. Envision these goals as already achieved, embracing the accompanying joy.
5. Affix Your Pieces: Once you're satisfied with the layout, glue or pin down the images and words to create a cohesive representation of your dreams.

6. Display Your Vision Board: Place your vision board in a prominent location in your home or workspace, serving as a daily reminder of your aspirations and your commitment to manifesting them.
7. Engage with Your Board: Regularly connect with your vision board. Visualize yourself achieving these dreams, immersing yourself in the feelings of fulfillment and happiness. This practice will help solidify your goals in your subconscious.

Aligning Goals with Your True Desires

As you embark on this visioning journey, ensure your goals reflect your true desires rather than societal expectations. Often, we pursue what others deem successful, overlooking our genuine aspirations. To ensure your goals resonate with your authentic self, consider these reflective questions:

- What brings me joy?
- What are my passions?
- What do I want my life to look like in 5, 10, or 20 years?
- If fear were not a factor, what would I pursue?

These questions will guide you toward a fulfilling life focused on what truly matters.

Maintaining Motivation and Focus on Long-Term Goals

Maintaining motivation and focus is essential as you visualize and pursue your radiant life. Here are strategies to help you stay on track:

1. Set Milestones: Break your long-term goals into smaller, actionable steps. Celebrate your progress at each milestone to keep your motivation high.
2. Daily Affirmations: Use positive affirmations to remind yourself of your vision and reinforce your belief in your ability to achieve it. Repeating these affirmations daily can help cultivate a growth mindset.
3. Create a Routine: Incorporate visualization and goal-setting into your daily routine. Consistency is key to keeping your dreams at the forefront of your mind.
4. Surround Yourself with Positivity: Engage with supportive communities or individuals who share your aspirations. Their encouragement can be a powerful motivator when challenges arise.
5. Reflect and Adjust: Periodically review your goals and progress. If needed, adjust your plans to stay aligned with your evolving vision and desires.

Overcoming Common Obstacles in Visualization

While visualization can be a powerful tool, it is not without its challenges. Here are some common obstacles you may encounter and tips for overcoming them:

1. Self-Doubt: It's normal to experience doubt, but recognizing it is the first step to overcoming it. Challenge negative thoughts with evidence of your past successes and remind yourself of your capabilities.
2. Lack of Clarity: If you struggle to visualize your goals, take time to reflect and refine them. Journaling can help clarify your thoughts and desires, making it easier to create a vivid mental picture.
3. Distractions: In our fast-paced world, distractions can derail your focus. Set aside dedicated time for visualization, free from interruptions, to immerse yourself in the practice.
4. Fear of Failure: The fear of not achieving your dreams can be paralyzing. Embrace the idea that failure is part of growth. Each setback provides valuable lessons that bring you closer to your goals.
5. Inconsistency: Consistency is vital for visualization to be effective. Establish regular practice, whether through daily visualization sessions or weekly reviews of your vision board, to reinforce your commitment.

Embracing the Journey

As you visualize your radiant life, remember that the journey toward your dreams is just as important as the destination. Each step you take contributes to manifesting the life you desire.

Inspired by Terri Savelle Foy, I hope to empower you to dream boldly and unapologetically.

Your dreams are valid and worth pursuing. Let your vision board guide you and remind you of the extraordinary life you are creating. Embrace the art of visioning, allowing it to illuminate your path as you turn your aspirations into reality.

However, it's crucial to balance those big dreams with practical, achievable goals to avoid disillusionment. Dream boldly, but ensure your action steps feel within reach. Set milestones that are realistic, allowing for progress without overwhelming yourself.

And just like Terri would say, "If you can dream it, you can do it!"—the self-help version of "Just do it!" but with a sprinkle of glitter and enthusiasm! So go ahead, grab those pom-poms, and let's cheer for all the dreams waiting to unfold!

Vision Boards of the Influential: Bringing Their Dreams to Life

The power of vision boards extends beyond personal journeys; many renowned individuals have harnessed this practice to shape their destinies. One inspiring example is Oprah Winfrey, who has openly discussed how vision boards have played a pivotal role in her life. Oprah attributes part of her success to visualization, famously stating that she would clip images from magazines representing her dreams and aspirations. By surrounding herself with these tangible reminders, she manifested her goals, from her television career to her philanthropic efforts. Her vision boards served as daily affirmations of her dreams, guiding her through challenges and reminding her of her path.

Another remarkable figure is Jim Carrey, who used visualization to propel himself into Hollywood. Early in his career, Carrey wrote himself a check for $10 million for "acting services rendered," dated it for Thanksgiving 1995. He kept this check in his wallet and visualized himself receiving such an amount for his work. Remarkably, he received a role in "Dumb and Dumber" that paid him $10 million, bringing his vision to life. Carrey's story exemplifies the extraordinary potential of combining visualization with unwavering belief in one's dreams.

By sharing these examples of influential figures like Oprah and Jim Carrey, we see tangible proof of how vision boards can turn aspirations into reality. Their journeys serve as powerful reminders that visualization can lead to real-life achievements. As you embark on creating your vision board, let their stories inspire and motivate you to dream boldly and manifest your own radiant life.

CHAPTER 10
Goal Setting with Heart and Purpose

"Setting goals is the first step in turning the invisible into the visible." — Tony Robbins

In the previous chapter, we discussed vision boarding as a creative way to visualize your dreams and aspirations. A vision board serves as a physical reminder of what you want to achieve, filled with inspiring images and words. It encourages you to imagine possibilities and create a visual representation of your ideal future.

In contrast, goal setting is a more structured method. It involves defining clear, measurable objectives that guide your actions as you work toward your vision. While vision boarding focuses on dreaming and visualizing your future, goal setting breaks those dreams down into actionable steps.

Both vision boards and goal setting are crucial parts of your journey toward radiance. Vision boards spark your imagination and passion, allowing you to see the bigger picture. On the other hand, goal setting provides a framework to help you turn those dreams into reality. Together, they create a powerful combination: vision boards inspire you, while goal setting keeps you focused and accountable. By using both tools, you can align your ambitions with your true desires, ensuring that every step you take resonates with your heart's purpose.

Many people view goal setting as a roadmap to success, a way to navigate toward their achievements. However, in my own journey toward radiance, I've learned that effective goal setting is more than just ambition; it's about connecting with your heart's deepest desires and purpose.

Discovering Your Deeper Calling

To set goals that resonate with your soul, it's vital to explore what truly drives you. Take time to reflect on your core values and passions. Ask yourself:

- What truly brings me joy?
- What are my non-negotiables in life?
- What legacy do I want to leave?

By exploring these questions, you will gain clarity about your life's purpose, which will serve as the foundation for your goals, ensuring they align with who you truly are.

The Importance of Aligning Goals with Personal Values

Aligning your goals with your personal values is essential for long-term fulfillment. When your goals reflect what is truly important to you, they become a source of motivation rather than obligation. For instance, if one of your core values is community, a goal to volunteer regularly or to start a community project can invigorate your spirit and drive your actions.

Consider the story of a woman named Maria whose core value is creativity. She spent years working in a corporate job that stifled her artistic instincts. After reflecting on her values, she set a goal to transition into a career in graphic design. By aligning her professional goals with her passion for creativity, Maria found renewed energy and enthusiasm in her work, ultimately leading to a successful and fulfilling career.

Breaking Down Long-Term Goals into Actionable Steps

Long-term goals can often feel overwhelming, making it essential to break them down into smaller, manageable steps. This process simplifies your path and helps maintain your motivation. Here's a structured approach to deconstructing your long-term goals:

1. Identify the Long-Term Goal: Start by clearly defining what you want to achieve in the long run. For example, "I want to write a book within the next three years."

2. Set Milestones: Break this goal into smaller milestones that can be achieved in a shorter timeframe. For instance:

- Write an outline by the end of month one.
- Complete the first draft by the end of year one.
- Edit and revise by the end of year two.

3. Outline Actionable Steps: For each milestone, list specific,

actionable steps. For example, under "Write an outline," you might include:

- Research similar books.
- Create character profiles.
- Develop a chapter-by-chapter overview.

4. Establish a Timeline: Assign deadlines to each milestone and step. This not only helps you stay on track but also gives you a sense of urgency.

5. Evaluate Progress: Regularly review your progress toward each milestone. Adjust your action steps as needed, ensuring they still align with your values and purpose.

6. Celebrate Small Wins: Acknowledge and celebrate the completion of each milestone. This practice keeps you motivated and reminds you of your progress toward the larger goal.

Goal-Setting Challenges and How to Overcome Them

While goal setting can be empowering, it also comes with its own set of challenges. Here are some common hurdles and strategies to overcome them:

- Fear of Failure: Many people hesitate to set ambitious goals due to the fear of not achieving them. To combat this, reframe failure as a learning opportunity. Embrace a growth mindset that values progress over perfection.
- Lack of Clarity: Sometimes, individuals struggle to define what they truly want. Engage in self-reflection and exploration of your values, passions, and aspirations to gain clearer insights.
- Overwhelm: Large goals can feel daunting. Break them down into smaller, actionable steps, as discussed earlier, to reduce feelings of overwhelm and create a sense of control.
- Distractions and Procrastination: Life can be full of distractions that pull you away from your goals. Create a dedicated space for goal-related work and establish a routine that prioritizes your objectives.
- Lack of Support: Surround yourself with a supportive community. Share your goals with friends or join groups that align with your aspirations. Accountability can significantly enhance your motivation.

Goal-Setting Workbook Section

To aid your goal-setting journey, I've included a workbook section with templates to help articulate your aspirations:

- Short-Term Goals (1-3 months)
- Goal: _____

  _____

- Action Steps:

  _____

  _____

- Deadline:

  _____

  _____

- Why is this important to me?

  _____

  _____

- Medium-Term Goals (6 months - 1 year)
- Goal: _____

  _____

- Action Steps:

  _____

  _____

- Deadline:

  _____

  _____

- Why is this important to me?

  _____

  _____

- Long-Term Goals (1-5 years)
- Goal:

  _____

  _____

- Action Steps:

  _____

  _____

- Deadline:

  _____

  _____

- Why is this important to me?

  _____

  _____

Use these templates to craft your goals and track your progress. Remember, it's not just about achieving outcomes but enjoying the journey of growth and self-discovery along the way. Aligning your goals with your heart and purpose is the key to creating a fulfilling life.

_____

_____

_____

_____

_____

_____

CHAPTER 11
Overcoming Fear and Building Resilience

"Do one thing every day that scares you." – Eleanor Roosevelt

Fear is a powerful emotion that can act as both a shield and a barrier. While it can protect us from danger, it often stands in the way of personal growth and self-discovery. Many of us experience fear when stepping out of our comfort zones, whether pursuing a new career, embarking on a relationship, or striving for a long-held dream. This chapter delves into the role of fear in hindering personal growth and offers practical techniques for overcoming it while emphasizing the importance of resilience in bouncing back from setbacks and relentlessly pursuing our goals.

Fear manifests in various forms—fear of failure, fear of judgment, fear of the unknown, and even fear of success. These anxieties can paralyze us, causing us to hesitate or abandon our aspirations altogether. When we let fear dictate our choices, we restrict our potential and limit the opportunities for growth that life presents. Recognizing that fear is a universal experience is the first step in dismantling its power over us. We are not alone in our fears; even the most successful individuals have faced their anxieties and doubts.

To overcome fear, we can employ several strategies:

1. Acknowledge Your Fear: The first step in overcoming fear is to recognize and accept it. Rather than suppressing or ignoring your feelings, take a moment to identify what specifically frightens you. Writing down your fears can also provide clarity and serve as a tangible reminder that they exist, but they do not define you.
2. Reframe Your Mindset: Shift your perspective by viewing fear as an opportunity for growth rather than a threat. Ask yourself what you can learn from facing your fears. This reframing can transform anxiety into motivation, encouraging you to take that first step forward.
3. Set Small, Achievable Goals: Breaking your larger goals into smaller, manageable steps can help alleviate feelings of overwhelm. Start with micro-actions that push you just outside your comfort zone. Each small achievement builds confidence and diminishes fear, creating a positive feedback loop that propels you to tackle bigger challenges.

4. Practice Mindfulness and Visualization: Engaging in mindfulness practices such as meditation can help you stay present and reduce anxiety. Visualization techniques can also be effective; imagine yourself succeeding and embracing the feelings of accomplishment and joy that come with it. This mental rehearsal can diminish fear and increase your readiness to act.
5. Seek Support: Surround yourself with a supportive network of friends, family, or mentors who encourage you to face your fears. Sharing your experiences can lighten the burden and provide you with new perspectives and insights.

Resilience plays a crucial role in overcoming fear and pursuing our goals. It is the ability to bounce back from setbacks and continue striving despite obstacles. Life is inherently unpredictable, and we will inevitably face challenges along our journey. Cultivating resilience helps us adapt and thrive in the face of adversity.

To build resilience, consider the following activities:

- Embrace a Growth Mindset: Adopt the belief that challenges and failures are opportunities for learning. This mindset fosters resilience by encouraging you to view difficulties as stepping stones rather than roadblocks.

- Develop Emotional Agility: Allow yourself to experience emotions, both positive and negative. Emotional agility involves acknowledging your feelings without letting them dictate your actions. This balance enables you to navigate through tough times with grace and determination.
- Establish a Routine of Self-Care: Taking care of your physical, emotional, and mental well-being is essential for resilience. Regular exercise, a balanced diet, and adequate rest are crucial. Additionally, engage in activities that bring you joy to replenish your spirit and fortify you against life's challenges.
- Reflect on Past Successes: Recall instances where you overcame difficulties and emerged stronger. Reflecting on your successes can remind you of your inner strength and reinforce your ability to handle future challenges.
- Practice Gratitude: Make it a habit to express gratitude daily. This can shift your focus from fear and challenges to the positive aspects of your life, enhancing your overall resilience.
- Engage in Creative Expression: Explore creative outlets such as writing, painting, or music. These activities can serve as therapeutic ways to process emotions and build resilience.
- Volunteer: Helping others can provide perspective and reinforce your sense of purpose. Engaging in

community service can also create connections that enhance your support network.

As you embrace the journey of overcoming fear and building resilience, remember that growth is a process. It requires patience, self-compassion, and a commitment to your goals. The path may be fraught with obstacles, but each step taken in the face of fear brings you closer to realizing your potential.

Reflective Questions:

1. What fears have held you back in the past, and how did they affect your journey?
2. How can you reframe your current fears into opportunities for growth?
3. What small steps can you take today to begin overcoming a specific fear?
4. Recall a time when you faced a setback. What did you learn from that experience, and how did it contribute to your resilience?
5. How can you nurture a supportive network that encourages you to face your fears and pursue your goals?

As you ponder these questions, remember that each moment of courage and resilience contributes to the radiance within you, illuminating the path toward your dreams.

CHAPTER 12
Manifestation in Action

"The future belongs to those who believe in the beauty of their dreams." — Eleanor Roosevelt

As I sit down to write this chapter, I can't help but reflect on all the moments that have shaped my understanding of manifestation. It's not merely about wishing for things or dreaming big; it's a deep, sometimes messy journey demanding faith, courage, and the strength to overcome doubt.

My journey with manifestation hasn't been a straight line. Many times, I felt lost, questioning whether I could trust the process or if my dreams were truly meant for me. I recall a particularly challenging period when uncertainty overwhelmed me. It felt like I was standing on the edge of a cliff, staring into a dark void filled with doubt. The fear of failure loomed large, casting shadows over my aspirations. Many nights, I would wake

MANIFESTATION IN ACTION

up with my heart racing, wondering if I was worthy of the life I envisioned.

In those vulnerable moments, I found comfort in my faith. I prayed for clarity, strength to face my insecurities, and guidance to take even the smallest steps forward. I cried and poured my heart out to God, seeking reassurance that I was on the right path. It was during these times of surrender that I began to understand the true power of belief. I learned that manifestation starts with trusting in something greater than myself—a divine force that knows my heart's desires, even when I waver.

A significant turning point in my journey was learning to visualize my goals as tangible realities, not just distant dreams. I created a vision board, a visual collection of my deepest aspirations. It featured images of places I wanted to visit, inspiring quotes, and representations of the life I wanted to build. Every time I looked at it, a spark of hope ignited within me, reminding me that I could manifest my dreams.

But let's be honest: it wasn't always easy. Doubt often crept in, making me question whether I was doing enough. I had to confront my limiting beliefs, realizing they were merely stories I had told myself for far too long. I remember a particularly tough day when I faced a setback in my career. It felt like a gut punch, and negativity threatened to wash over me. In those moments, it was tempting to abandon my vision board and my dreams entirely. Yet, I learned that resilience is nurtured in adversity.

With the unwavering support of my son, Liam, who observed my struggles with innocent curiosity, I knew I couldn't let my dreams fade away. I wanted him to see that pursuing a meaningful life takes grit and perseverance. I wanted him to understand that setbacks are merely stepping stones toward growth. As I wiped away my tears and gathered my strength, I made a pact with myself to keep moving forward, no matter how daunting the journey felt.

As I embraced the practice of manifestation, I began to see the tangible results of my efforts. I learned to take inspired action, even when fear gripped me. I started saying yes to opportunities that scared me and pushed me out of my comfort zone. Slowly, I began to witness the fruits of my labor—milestones I once thought were unreachable now felt within grasp.

I want you to understand that manifestation isn't just wishful thinking; it's a deliberate practice requiring faith and commitment. It involves setting intentions and aligning your actions with those intentions, even when the path ahead is unclear. I encourage you to create your affirmation practice. Write down affirmations that resonate with your desires—statements that remind you of your worth and the power within you. Repeat them daily, allowing them to anchor your belief in what you can achieve.

Embrace the beautiful dance between faith and action. Understand that the journey to manifesting your dreams may be filled with ups and downs, but every twist and turn brings you closer to the life you envision. Trust the process, lean into the discomfort, and remember that every step you take is a declaration of your commitment to living authentically.

The Power of Faith and Visualization

Faith is the cornerstone of manifestation—it's the

unwavering belief that you can achieve your dreams. Visualization enhances this faith, allowing you to see and feel your desires as if they are already your reality.

Throughout my journey, I found strength in visualization, especially during uncertain times. I would close my eyes and vividly picture my desired outcomes—the emotions I would feel and the details of my surroundings. This practice not only kept me motivated but also aligned my actions with my intentions.

The 5-Step Process

Manifestation is not merely about wishing for your desires; it's about actively engaging in the process. Here's how to navigate your own manifestation journey:

1. Clarify Your Intentions: Be specific about what you want to manifest. The clearer you are, the better you can align your actions.
2. Visualize with Emotion: Spend time each day visualizing your goals. Feel the joy, gratitude, and excitement of achieving your dreams. This emotional connection strengthens your manifestation practice.
3. Take Inspired Action: Manifestation requires movement. Stay open to opportunities that arise and take steps that resonate with your intentions. Small, consistent actions can lead to significant results.
4. Overcome Doubt: Doubt is a natural part of the journey. Combat negative thoughts with affirmations that reinforce your belief in your capabilities. It's okay to feel fear; just don't let it hold you back.

5. Trust the Process: Understand that the journey of manifestation may not always go as planned. Trust that every step, whether forward or backward, is part of your growth.

Creating Your Affirmation Practice

Affirmations are powerful tools that anchor your manifestations in belief. Here's how to create an effective affirmation practice:

1. Identify Key Affirmations: Choose affirmations that resonate with your goals. For example:

- "I am worthy of my dreams."
- "I attract abundance effortlessly."
- "I am aligned with my highest self."

2. Repeat Daily: Make it a habit to recite your affirmations every day, ideally in the morning and before bed. This repetition will help reinforce positive beliefs in your subconscious mind.

3. Visualize While Affirming: Combine visualization with your affirmations. As you recite them, picture your desires coming to life, deepening your emotional connection to your goals.

4. Stay Open to Signs: As you affirm and visualize, be receptive to the signs and opportunities that the universe presents. Sometimes, your manifestations may come in unexpected forms.

Embrace Your Manifestation Journey

MANIFESTATION IN ACTION

Manifestation is a dynamic process empowering you to create the life you desire. Embrace the journey with an open heart and mind, knowing that you are the architect of your dreams. Let faith, visualization, and aligned action guide you on this radiant path. With every step you take, you are not just dreaming; you are actively creating a life that reflects your true essence.

PART FOUR
Empowering Others Through Radiance

CHAPTER 13
Breaking Free from Limiting Beliefs

"Your belief determines your action and your action determines your results." — John Maxwell

Understanding Limiting Beliefs

Limiting beliefs are entrenched thoughts or assumptions that hinder our progress toward our goals. They often disguise themselves as truths, influencing our self-perception and worldview. These beliefs can stem from:

- Past Failures: Think of a time when you tried something and it didn't go well—like auditioning for a play and not getting the part. This might lead you to believe, "I'll never succeed in acting."

- Societal Conditioning: Consider someone in a family where no one has pursued higher education. They might think, "People like me don't go to college."
- Fear of Judgment: Picture a person hesitant to share their art because they fear criticism. They might think, "What will others think if I try and fail?"

Key Insight: Limiting beliefs are not absolute truths; they are narratives we've internalized. The empowering news is that we hold the ability to rewrite these narratives.

Identifying Your Limiting Beliefs

The first step to overcoming limiting beliefs is to bring them into the open. These beliefs often thrive in the recesses of our subconscious.

Reflection Exercise: Uncover Your Beliefs

Spend 10–15 minutes reflecting on these prompts:

1. What's holding me back? Identify a goal or dream you've been neglecting.
2. Why haven't I pursued it? Write down fears or doubts that come to mind.
3. What do I believe about myself in this context? Look for phrases like "I'm not good enough" or "I lack the time/money/skills."

Example:

- Goal: Start my own business.

- Reason for Inaction: "I fear failure and financial loss."
- Belief: "I'm not intelligent enough to be an entrepreneur."

Challenging and Reframing Limiting Beliefs

Once you've identified your limiting beliefs, it's time to challenge them. These beliefs seldom rest on objective truths.

Step 1: Question Their Validity

Ask yourself:

- Is this belief grounded in facts or merely assumptions?
- What evidence exists that contradicts this belief?
- How might I view this situation if fear were absent?

Example:

- Belief: "I'm not smart enough to be an entrepreneur."
- Challenge: "I've successfully managed complex projects and learned new skills as needed."
- Reframe: "I possess the intelligence and resourcefulness to start a business and adapt as necessary."

Step 2: Replace with Empowering Beliefs

Transform limiting beliefs into affirmations that inspire and empower you.

Exercise: Rewrite Your Narrative

Take a limiting belief and convert it into a positive, empowering statement.

1. Identify a belief that has constrained you.
2. Counter it with evidence of your capabilities.
3. Transform it into an uplifting statement.

Example:

- Limiting Belief: "I'm not creative enough to write a book."
- Counter Evidence: "I've received praise for my essays and have unique ideas to share."
- Empowering Statement: "I am a creative thinker with valuable stories to tell, and my writing will inspire others."

Building Confidence Through Action

Limiting beliefs often breed a fear of failure. The most effective way to combat this fear is through action. Taking small, consistent steps can build momentum and bolster your confidence.

Action Plan:

1. Start Small: Break your goal into manageable steps.

- Example: If your goal is to start a business, begin by researching your industry or drafting a simple business plan.

1. Celebrate Progress: Acknowledge and reward yourself for each step, however minor.

- Example: Completing your first chapter or sharing your idea with a friend.

1. Embrace Failure as Growth: View setbacks as opportunities for learning.

- Mantra: "Each failure brings me closer to success."

Guided Visualization: Breaking Free

Close your eyes and envision a limiting belief as a heavy chain restraining you. Now, visualize yourself breaking that chain:

1. See yourself taking small, purposeful steps toward your goal.
2. Imagine achieving it, feeling the joy and pride of that moment.
3. Affirm: "I am free from limiting beliefs. I am capable and deserving of success."

Affirmation Practice

Incorporate a daily affirmation routine to reinforce your new beliefs:

- Morning Ritual: Write or recite affirmations like:
- "I am worthy of success."
- "I release all doubts and embrace my potential."
- Evening Reflection: Journal about one action you took that day to confront a limiting belief.

Your Path to Freedom

Overcoming limiting beliefs is a journey that requires time and persistence, but with mindfulness and consistent action, you can liberate yourself. Every forward step is a victory, and each belief you reframe is a testament to your power.

Final Reflection:

- What belief will you challenge today?
- What one small action can you take right now to move toward your goal?

Remember: The only limits that truly exist are the ones you accept. Rewrite your narrative, reclaim your strength, and boldly embrace your radiant future.

CHAPTER 14
The Power of Renewal

"Every day is a new beginning. Take a deep breath, smile, and start again." — Claritza Rausch Peralta

Renewal is the process of letting go of what no longer serves us and embracing new opportunities for growth. Just as spring brings new growth after winter, renewal allows us to bloom after periods of stagnation. It is a transformative cycle, much like the changing seasons, where we shed the old to make way for the new.

Renewal has become a cornerstone of my life—a constant source of strength and resilience that empowers me to embrace new phases with grace and confidence. People often ask me, "Why are you always so happy and radiant?" The truth is, my journey to joy was not instantaneous; it took time, reflection, and a commitment to the art of renewal.

Exploring Different Paths to Renewal

While personal stories of transformation are compelling, renewal can manifest in various forms and paths. Each individual may find their unique journey influenced by their circumstances, aspirations, and environment. Here, we will explore different paths to renewal that extend beyond individual narratives.

Community Engagement and Connection

One powerful path to renewal lies in community engagement. Becoming involved in local initiatives or volunteering can provide a renewed sense of purpose. For example, participating in community clean-up events or mentoring youth can foster connections and inspire change—not only in the community but within oneself. The act of giving back often leads to personal growth and a sense of belonging, reinforcing the idea that renewal is a collective experience.

Creative Expression

Creative arts can serve as a profound means of renewal. Whether through painting, writing, music, or dance, expressing oneself creatively allows for the exploration of emotions and experiences that may otherwise remain unvoiced. Engaging in creative activities can provide a cathartic release, offering a fresh perspective on one's life and circumstances. Many individuals find that immersing themselves in artistic endeavors enables them to process their experiences, paving the way for renewal.

Spiritual Exploration

For some, spiritual exploration offers a robust path to renewal. This journey may involve connecting with nature, practicing mindfulness, or exploring different spiritual traditions.

Engaging in practices such as meditation or yoga can facilitate introspection and foster a deeper understanding of oneself. Spiritual renewal often provides clarity, enabling individuals to realign their values and beliefs, which can significantly impact their outlook on life.

Education and Lifelong Learning

Pursuing education and lifelong learning can also be a transformative path to renewal. Whether through formal education, workshops, or self-directed study, acquiring new knowledge and skills can invigorate one's life. This pursuit not only enhances professional prospects but can also lead to personal enrichment and a renewed sense of curiosity. Embracing the idea of being a lifelong learner encourages adaptability and growth, essential components of the renewal process.

Mindful Living

The practice of mindful living is another avenue for renewal. By cultivating awareness of the present moment, individuals can let go of past regrets and future anxieties, creating space for new experiences. Mindfulness can be integrated into daily routines, transforming mundane tasks into opportunities for reflection and appreciation. This shift towards a mindful approach can lead to a more profound sense of peace and fulfillment.

Rituals and Traditions

Establishing personal rituals or honoring traditions can also facilitate renewal. Whether celebrating seasonal changes, marking significant life events, or creating new family traditions, these practices can ground individuals in their identities and foster a sense of continuity amidst change. Rituals provide a framework for reflection, allowing individuals to honor their past while embracing future possibilities.

Reframing Challenges as Opportunities

Lastly, reframing challenges as opportunities for growth can be a crucial aspect of renewal. Life inevitably presents obstacles; however, viewing these challenges through a lens of possibility can transform how one navigates difficulties. This perspective encourages resilience and adaptability, fostering a mindset that embraces change rather than resisting it. By recognizing that every challenge carries the potential for renewal, individuals can cultivate a more empowering narrative of their lives.

To effectively manage setbacks such as losing motivation or balancing multiple goals, consider implementing a weekly review habit. This practice allows you to reflect on your progress, celebrate small victories, and identify areas that need adjustment. By dedicating time each week to evaluate your goals and challenges, you can maintain focus and motivation, ensuring that you stay on track even when faced with difficulties. Additionally, setting specific, manageable goals for each week can help create a sense of accomplishment and momentum, making it easier to navigate the ups and downs of your journey.

Embracing the Journey of Renewal

As we explore these diverse paths to renewal, it becomes evident that each journey is unique and multifaceted. While personal stories inspire us, the broader landscape of renewal encompasses community connections, creative expression, spiritual growth, education, mindful living, rituals, and the reframing of challenges. Each path offers its own set of opportunities for transformation, inviting us to embrace change in myriad ways.

In your journey, remember that renewal is not a one-time event but an ongoing process. By remaining open to new experiences and perspectives, you can continually redefine your story and cultivate resilience.

It is crucial to ensure that your goals reflect your personal values. Pursuing achievements that do not align with what truly matters to you can lead to feelings of emptiness and dissatisfaction. Taking the time to clarify your values can help you avoid chasing hollow accomplishments and instead guide you toward pursuits that bring genuine fulfillment.

Embrace the power of renewal in all its forms, and allow it to guide you toward a vibrant, meaningful life.

Reflective Exercises

To deepen your understanding of your own journey toward renewal, consider these journaling prompts:

1. What area of your life feels stagnant, and how can you invite renewal into it?
2. What's one habit, thought, or relationship you can release to make space for growth?
3. Which path to renewal—community, creativity, spirituality, or education—resonates most with you, and why?

Readiness for Renewal Checklist

Assess your readiness for renewal by reflecting on the following questions:

- Am I holding onto past beliefs or habits that no longer serve me?
- Have I taken the time to clarify my personal values?
- Am I open to new experiences and perspectives?
- Do I feel a sense of fulfillment in my current pursuits?
- What steps can I take today to begin my journey of renewal?

Use these reflections to guide your path forward and embrace the transformative power of renewal in your life.

CHAPTER 15
The Art of Leadership and Influence

"The function of leadership is to produce more leaders, not more followers." — Ralph Nader

There was a moment in my life when fear almost paralyzed me—my fear of public speaking. The thought of standing in front of an audience, with all eyes on me, filled me with dread. When the opportunity arose to share my book at my church, a wave of panic washed over me. The idea of speaking about something so personal in front of my community was daunting.

However, I realized that this was more than just a chance to promote my book; it was an opportunity to connect with others on a deeper level. My desire to share my story and the message woven into my book became my motivation. I imagined how my words could resonate with someone in the audience, inspire them, or uplift their spirits. This thought pushed me to take action despite my fear.

On the day of the talk, as I stood at the podium, my heart raced, and my palms felt clammy. But as I began to speak, I noticed the faces in the crowd—some were nodding, while others appeared visibly moved. I shared my journey, the struggles I faced, and the lessons I learned. To my surprise, my vulnerability opened a channel of empathy and connection. By the end of my speech, I saw tears in many eyes, including my own.

That moment taught me that stepping into our fears can lead to profound experiences. The emotional response from my audience reminded me that sharing our stories creates powerful bonds. It was worth overcoming my fear of that connection. I walked away feeling empowered, knowing that I had faced my fear, and it had led to something beautiful.

Great leaders are defined by their empathy, integrity, and clear vision. These traits build strong relationships and create an atmosphere where everyone feels valued and motivated to give their best.

To be an effective leader, it's essential to lead by example. Your actions speak louder than words; they set the standard for your entire team. When you demonstrate commitment, resilience, and a strong work ethic, you inspire your team to embody those same qualities. It's not enough to assign tasks; you must actively participate in the work, demonstrating that you are all in this together. This shared experience fosters trust and accountability among team members.

Having a motivating vision is also key to successful

leadership. A clear, compelling vision provides direction and purpose, helping team members understand the "why" behind their work. When individuals see how their contributions fit into the bigger picture, they feel a deeper sense of investment. A good leader consistently communicates this vision, weaving it into daily conversations and decisions so it remains a guiding force for the team.

Additionally, effective leadership is an ongoing journey of inspiration. Regularly checking in with your team, seeking their input, and celebrating their achievements can create a strong sense of belonging. It's crucial to foster an environment where everyone feels comfortable sharing their ideas and feedback. This collaborative spirit not only sparks creativity but also strengthens the bonds among team members.

Reflective Questions:

1. How do my actions reflect the values I want to instill in my team?
2. How can I better share and communicate my vision with my team?
3. What practices can I adopt to promote open communication and collaboration?
4. How do I celebrate my team's successes to keep their motivation high?

CHAPTER 16
Inspiring Others Through Your Story

"The only way to truly be happy is to make others happy." — Joyce Meyer

One of the most fulfilling aspects of personal growth is our ability to inspire and uplift those around us.

I still vividly remember when someone first reached out to me, sharing how my story had impacted her life. I had just finished recounting my journey of overcoming challenges on social media when I received a message that changed everything for me.

She wrote, "Thank you for sharing your story. It's truly inspiring. I've been struggling for a long time, and hearing how you turned your pain into purpose gave me hope." As I read her words, I felt a rush of emotions. I had always believed in the power of storytelling, but in that moment, I understood just how deeply my experiences could resonate with others.

When women write to me, expressing their thoughts and feelings about my journey, I sometimes find myself at a loss for words. It can be overwhelming to realize that my life's narrative touches others so profoundly. That day in the coffee shop became a pivotal moment for me; it reminded me that our stories are not solely our own. They are part of a larger human experience, capable of encouraging others to embark on their own paths of healing and growth.

Reflecting on this, I realize that the true reward of personal growth extends beyond our own transformations. It lies in our ability to uplift those around us. My journey of healing and empowerment has become a launching pad, enabling me to show up authentically in the world and inspire others to thrive. Each connection and every shared story reinforces the idea that we are all part of a community, navigating life's challenges and triumphs together.

My journey toward radiance didn't just end with my own healing; it opened the door for me to help others embrace their own light. In this chapter, we will explore the profound impact we can have when we show up authentically in the world, paving the way for others to flourish.

The Ripple Effect of Authenticity

When I began living authentically and sharing my story of struggle and triumph, I noticed how my openness invited others to do the same. Vulnerability is contagious; it encourages people to shed their masks and reveal their true selves. I started receiving messages from friends and acquaintances who were touched by my journey—people expressing gratitude for the courage I exhibited and how it inspired them to confront their challenges.

This ripple effect reminds us that our journeys are interconnected. When we choose to embrace our truth, we empower those around us to do the same. By being authentic, we create an atmosphere where others feel safe to express their vulnerabilities and aspirations.

Becoming a Source of Inspiration and Support

In this chapter, I want to emphasize the importance of becoming a beacon of inspiration for others. Whether you find yourself in a mentorship role, as a supportive friend, or as a leader in your community, several ways to foster growth in those around you include:

1. Listen Actively: Be present for others. Sometimes, people just need someone to listen without judgment. Create an open space where they can share their thoughts and feelings freely.
2. Share Your Story: Your experiences hold power. Share your journey, the obstacles you've faced, and the lessons you've learned. Authentic storytelling fosters connection and understanding.

3. Encourage and Empower: Use your voice to uplift others. Offer encouragement and support, especially during difficult times. Remind them of their strengths and capabilities.
4. Celebrate Progress: Acknowledge and celebrate the milestones, big or small, that others achieve. Recognizing their progress boosts their confidence and motivates them to continue striving for their goals.

Building a Community of Growth and Empowerment

Creating a supportive community is essential for fostering collective growth. Here are some strategies to help you build a safe space for others to thrive:

1. Create Safe Spaces: Organize gatherings, workshops, or support groups where individuals can come together to share, learn, and grow. Ensure these spaces are judgment-free zones where everyone feels valued.
2. Lead by Example: Model the behavior you wish to see in others. Demonstrate the importance of self-care, authenticity, and growth in your own life, inspiring others to follow suit.
3. Encourage Collaboration: Facilitate opportunities for people to work together, share their gifts, and learn from one another. Collaborative efforts create a sense of belonging and community.

4. Emphasize Lifelong Learning: Promote the idea that growth is a continuous journey. Encourage individuals to pursue new experiences, skills, and knowledge, reinforcing that learning never stops.

The Joy of Empowering Others

One of the greatest joys of my journey has been witnessing others shine. I've seen friends take bold steps toward their dreams, mentors inspire their protégés, and leaders cultivate environments where everyone can flourish. Each time someone steps into their power, it reaffirms my belief in the transformative nature of our connections.

As you embark on this journey of helping others radiate, remember that your light can ignite the flames of inspiration in those around you. Embrace your role as a source of support and encouragement, knowing that your authenticity can create waves of positive change.

Reflective Exercises:

- What's one experience in your life that taught you resilience? Take a moment to think about a challenging situation you faced and how it shaped you.
- How can sharing this experience help others? Consider the lessons learned and how your story might resonate with someone else who is struggling.
- What steps can you take to start inspiring others today? Identify one action you can take, whether it's

INSPIRING OTHERS THROUGH YOUR STORY

reaching out to someone in need, sharing your story, or simply being a supportive presence in someone's life.

By reflecting on these prompts, you can connect with your own journey and discover ways to empower others to shine just as brightly.

CHAPTER 17
Building Trust and Effective Communication

"The most important thing in communication is hearing what isn't said." – Peter Drucker

In this chapter, I want to share my personal journey with communication, which has always been a challenge for me. As I learned about building trust and forming real connections, I discovered that communication is more than just speaking well; it's about truly understanding each other. This exploration pushed me to face my fears and limitations, turning them into chances for growth.

I remember a time when I found it hard to share my feelings during an argument with someone I cared about. My fear of saying the wrong thing made the silence feel overwhelming, adding to the tension between us. I realized that every unspoken word created distance, highlighting how important effective communication is for connecting with others. That tough moment became a turning point for me, helping me learn not only about the mechanics of communication but also about the deeper emotions that influence our interactions.

As I examined trust, communication, and connection, I found that my struggles were not unique. Many people face the challenge of expressing their feelings and thoughts clearly, which often leads to misunderstandings and feelings of loneliness. Instead of building connections, I was unintentionally creating barriers because I was afraid to be vulnerable.

Through my journey toward better communication, I learned that it's not just about the words we use; it's also about the intentions behind those words. Listening—truly listening—is as vital as speaking. This insight changed how I approached my relationships. I began to see that trust is developed through open conversations, where everyone feels safe to share their true selves without fear of being judged.

In the complex world of human relationships, trust, and effective communication are the essential threads that hold us together. These elements are not just extras; they are the foundation that supports understanding, respect, and love. To build strong relationships, we need to invest time and effort into nurturing trust and communication. By doing this, we can create a safe space for open dialogue, ultimately strengthening our connections with one another.

Building Trust

Trust is the cornerstone of every relationship—be it romantic, familial, or platonic. It develops over time through consistent actions, honesty, and vulnerability. Here are some strategies to help foster trust:

1. Be Transparent: Share your thoughts and feelings openly. When you express your true self, it encourages others to do the same.
2. Honor Your Commitments: Follow through on promises, no matter how small. Reliability builds a sense of security in the relationship.
3. Practice Empathy: Try to see situations from the other person's perspective. Understanding their feelings will deepen your connection and establish trust.
4. Show Appreciation: Acknowledge the efforts and qualities of the other person. Gratitude strengthens bonds and reinforces trust.
5. Be Consistent: Consistency in your words and actions reinforces trust. When others can predict how you will respond, they feel more secure in the relationship.
6. Admit Mistakes: When you err, acknowledge it openly. Taking responsibility for your actions demonstrates integrity and fosters a culture of honesty.
7. Be Vulnerable: Share your fears and insecurities. This not only humanizes you but also invites the other person to open up in return.

Effective Communication

Effective communication is more than just exchanging words; it involves understanding and being understood. Here are practical tips for enhancing communication:

1. Active Listening: Focus entirely on the speaker. Avoid interrupting, and show that you are engaged through nodding or affirming sounds. This demonstrates respect and encourages openness.
2. Clarify and Reflect: Paraphrase what the other person has said to ensure understanding. This not only shows that you are listening but also helps clarify any misunderstandings.
3. Nonverbal Cues: Pay attention to body language, tone of voice, and facial expressions. Nonverbal communication often conveys more than words alone.
4. Encourage Open Dialogue: Create a safe space for sharing thoughts and feelings. Assure the other person that you value their input, even if it differs from your own.
5. Use "I" Statements: Frame your thoughts from your perspective by using "I" statements. This reduces defensiveness and opens the door for healthy dialogue.
6. Ask Open-Ended Questions: Encourage deeper conversations by posing questions that require more

than a yes or no answer. This fosters exploration and understanding.
7. Provide Constructive Feedback: When offering feedback, focus on behaviors rather than personal attributes. This helps maintain a positive tone and encourages growth.

Conflict Resolution

Conflicts are a natural part of any relationship, but how we handle them can either strengthen or weaken our bonds. Here are techniques for resolving conflicts effectively:

1. Stay Calm: Approach conflicts with a level head. Take a moment to breathe and collect your thoughts before responding.
2. Focus on the Issue: Address the specific problem rather than bringing up past grievances. This keeps the discussion constructive and prevents escalation.
3. Seek Solutions Together: Collaborate on finding a resolution that satisfies both parties. This fosters teamwork and reinforces trust.
4. Agree to Disagree: Sometimes, it's okay not to see eye to eye. Acknowledge differing viewpoints and respect the other person's perspective.
5. Use Time-Outs if Necessary: If emotions run high, it's okay to take a break to cool down. This can prevent saying things in anger that might be regretted later.

Building Trust and Effective Communication

Fostering Open Dialogue

Creating an environment where open dialogue is encouraged is crucial for maintaining trust and effective communication. Here are some reflective questions to guide you:

- How do I express my feelings and thoughts in my relationships?
- What are my triggers in conflicts, and how can I manage them better?
- Do I listen actively, or do I find myself distracted during conversations?
- How can I demonstrate gratitude and appreciation more often?
- What steps can I take to ensure my partner or friend feels heard and valued?

Communication Tools and Resources

To enhance your communication skills, consider incorporating the following tools and resources into your practice:

1. Books: Explore titles focused on communication skills, such as "Nonviolent Communication" by Marshall Rosenberg or "Crucial Conversations" by Kerry Patterson et al. These offer practical insights and techniques.
2. Workshops: Attend workshops or seminars on effective communication and conflict resolution.

These can provide hands-on practice and expert guidance.
3. Online Courses: Utilize platforms like Coursera or Udemy to find courses dedicated to improving communication skills. Many courses offer interactive components to practice what you learn.
4. Apps: Consider using apps that focus on mindfulness and emotional intelligence, such as Headspace or Moodfit. These can help you become more aware of your feelings and reactions during conversations.
5. Journaling: Keep a communication journal to reflect on your interactions. Writing down your thoughts can help identify patterns and improve your responses.

As you navigate the complex world of relationships, remember that building trust and effective communication is an ongoing journey. By implementing these strategies and remaining open to growth and understanding, you will cultivate deeper, more meaningful connections with those around you. Trust and communication may take time to develop, but the rewards are immeasurable, illuminating the path to a more fulfilling existence.

CHAPTER 18
The Radiance Within

Imagine standing in a dark room, the silence pressing against you like a heavy blanket. Suddenly, you strike a match, and in an instant, that small flame flickers to life. It dances and casts warm, golden shadows on the walls, illuminating corners that were once shrouded in darkness. This tiny light, seemingly insignificant, transforms the atmosphere, revealing the beauty and detail that was always there but hidden from view.

Just like that flame, your radiance has the power to light up not only your own life but also the lives of those around you. Each of us carries an inner glow, waiting to be recognized and embraced. As we draw the curtains on this transformative journey, let's take a moment to celebrate what it truly means to live a radiant life from within.

Living radiantly is about more than just positive energy; it's about the essence of who you are. It's the unique blend of your passions, strengths, and values that creates a light no one else can replicate. When you acknowledge and nurture this inner glow, you begin to shine brighter, illuminating the path for others as well.

So, what does it mean to embrace your essence? It starts with self-acceptance—recognizing your worth and the unique gifts you bring to the world. When you stand confidently in your truth, you radiate a warmth that draws others in, creating connections that are both profound and uplifting.

As you move forward, remember that each step you take toward embracing your radiance doesn't just benefit you; it has a ripple effect. Like the flickering flame that expands to fill a room, your light can inspire those around you to ignite their own inner fire. Together, we can create a world where everyone's brilliance is celebrated and the shadows of doubt and fear are banished.

In this chapter, I invite you to reflect on your own light. What are the qualities that make you shine? How can you nurture them further? Embrace the journey of self-discovery and watch as your radiance transforms not just your life but also the lives of those you touch. Let your light be a beacon, guiding others through their own darkness, reminding them that they, too, possess the power to illuminate their world

Embracing Your Evolving Journey

Living a radiant life is not a destination—it's a beautiful, ongoing process. Each of us holds a unique light, capable of shining through the shadows of life. To live radiantly is to honor every facet of your journey, accepting both the joyous peaks and the challenging valleys. Every experience, whether uplifting or painful, contributes to the masterpiece of who you are becoming.

Your story is remarkable in its authenticity. The trials you've faced have forged your strength, and the lessons learned have deepened your wisdom. Remember, your worth is not determined by external accolades but by the love, kindness, and truth you cultivate within yourself.

Recognizing Your Radiance and Potential

You are a radiant being, filled with potential just waiting to be unleashed. Embracing this truth is essential; it shapes your thoughts, actions, and dreams. When you view yourself through the lens of love and acceptance, you tap into a power that transcends limitations.

The world eagerly awaits your light. Your unique gifts have the capacity to inspire and uplift those around you. Embrace your individuality and let your authentic self shine unapologetically. There is no one else like you, and that is your superpower.

A Vision for Your Future

I invite you to engage in a reflective exercise that will help you connect with your future self and commit to your continued growth and radiance.

1. Write a Letter to Your Future Self
2. Find a quiet space and take out your journal. Allow your thoughts to flow as you write a heartfelt letter to your future self. Here are some detailed prompts to guide your writing:
3. Acknowledge Your Growth: Reflect on your journey and celebrate how far you've come. Consider both the small and large victories you've achieved. You might write something like, "Dear Future Me, I am so proud of the courage you've shown in pursuing your dreams. Remember how you embraced challenges and grew stronger with each step?"
4. Set Intentions: What do you hope to achieve in the coming years? How do you want to feel? Write about the radiance you wish to embody and the dreams you wish to pursue. You could include thoughts like, "I hope you've continued to trust in your brilliance and fueled your passions. I wish for you to be surrounded by positivity and to pursue your dreams fearlessly."
5. Commit to Your Journey: Make a promise to yourself to prioritize personal growth, embrace challenges, and nurture the radiance within. You might express, "I commit to nurturing my creativity and believing in

my abilities. I promise to be kind to myself and to take risks that lead to growth."
6. Additional Prompts: To deepen your reflection, consider these questions:
7. What advice would your future self give you now?
8. What are the key milestones you hope to achieve in the next year?
9. How do you envision your life in five years?
10. What fears do you want to overcome, and how can you start addressing them today?
11. Seal and Revisit: Once you've finished your letter, seal it in an envelope and date it. Set a reminder to revisit it in six months or a year. Let this letter serve as a guiding light, reminding you of your intentions and dreams. When you open it, reflect on your growth and celebrate the journey you've undertaken.

By engaging in this exercise, you cultivate a deeper connection with your aspirations and reinforce a commitment to your personal growth.

Embrace Your Radiance

As you enter this new phase of your life, remember that the brilliance within you is an eternal flame. Nurture it with self-love, compassion, and decisive action. Embrace your journey with an open heart, knowing that you are capable of achieving extraordinary things.

Let your light shine brightly—not just for your own benefit but also for those around you. Illuminate the paths of others, creating a ripple effect of inspiration and empowerment. Together, we can foster a world that celebrates radiance, encouraging everyone to embrace their authentic selves.

Radiance isn't merely a fleeting moment of joy or a temporary state; it's a lifelong commitment to honoring your true self. It's about recognizing your worthiness of love, happiness, and success. Each day, as you step into the world, carry the understanding that your light has the power to inspire those around you. Your journey is not just for you; it serves as a beacon for others who may feel lost in their own darkness.

I encourage you to embrace this light and let it shine with all its brilliance. Share your story, your struggles, and your triumphs. Become a source of inspiration for someone seeking a guiding star. The world needs your unique voice, your experiences, and your insights. Let your radiance ripple out, creating waves of positivity and empowerment.

Take bold steps toward your dreams. Whether through visualization, heartfelt intentions, or sharing your journey with others, remember that each day is a fresh opportunity to become the person you aspire to be. Be intentional, be courageous, and above all, be authentic.

I invite you to share your commitment to living radiantly with the world. Use the hashtag #TheRadianceWithin on your social media platforms to connect with others on their paths of self-discovery and empowerment. Share your insights, vision boards, and stories of transformation. Let's build a community where we uplift each other, celebrate our victories, and support one another through challenges.

THE RADIANCE WITHIN

By using #RadianceWithin, you not only honor your own journey but also inspire countless others to join this movement of self-love and empowerment. Together, we can create a powerful network of individuals committed to living their most radiant lives.

As you conclude this chapter of your journey, remember: You are enough. You are powerful. You are radiant.

Embrace this truth fully and let the world bask in your glow. The time is now; your journey to radiance starts today!

Reflection Prompts:

- What does living radiantly mean to you?
- How can you honor your journey and celebrate your unique gifts today?
- What steps will you take to nurture your inner light moving forward?

Take a moment to reflect on these questions and allow your thoughts to guide you toward embracing your true radiance.

PART FIVE

Nurturing Radiance in Relationships

CHAPTER 19

Building Radiant Connections

"The quality of your life is the quality of your relationships." — Tony Robbins

The journey to radiance is not one that we walk alone. Our relationships play a crucial role in shaping who we are and how we experience the world. In this chapter, we explore the importance of building connections that nurture and amplify our inner light.

Cultivating Meaningful Relationships

Meaningful relationships are the cornerstone of a fulfilling life. They provide support, love, and a sense of belonging. However, cultivating such relationships requires intention and effort. Here are some ways to build and enhance your connections:

1. **Be Present**: Show up fully in your interactions. Listen actively and engage with empathy, creating a space where others feel heard and valued.
2. **Communicate Openly**: Foster open and honest communication. Share your thoughts and feelings, and encourage others to do the same.
3. **Practice Gratitude**: Express appreciation for the people in your life. Acknowledge their contributions and let them know how much they mean to you.
4. **Set Healthy Boundaries**: Protect your energy by establishing boundaries that honor your needs while respecting those of others.
5. **Support Growth**: Encourage the personal growth of those around you. Celebrate their successes and stand by them through challenges.

Building a Supportive Community

While meaningful relationships form the foundation of our individual growth, building a supportive community expands that growth to a collective level. It's about creating spaces where people not only thrive but also uplift one another.

Creating a supportive community extends beyond individual relationships. It involves fostering a network of people who uplift and inspire one another. Consider these steps to build a nurturing community:

- Organize Gatherings: Host events or meetups where like-minded individuals can connect and share their experiences.
- Create Safe Spaces: Establish environments where people feel comfortable being their authentic selves without fear of judgment.
- Facilitate Collaboration: Encourage collaboration and mutual support. Create opportunities for people to work together and learn from one another.
- Celebrate Diversity: Embrace the unique qualities and perspectives each person brings. Celebrate diversity within your community and learn from different viewpoints.

CHAPTER 20
Healing Relationships Through Forgiveness

"Forgiveness does not change the past, but it does enlarge the future." — Paul Boese

Forgiveness is a powerful act that can heal wounds and restore harmony within relationships. In this chapter, we explore the transformative nature of forgiveness and how it can lead to deeper, more meaningful connections.

Understanding the challenges of forgiveness can help individuals navigate this process more effectively. Here are some common challenges faced during this journey:

1. **Resistance to Letting Go**: Many struggle with releasing anger and resentment, often believing that holding onto these feelings provides a sense of control. Overcoming this mindset requires

recognizing that forgiveness is ultimately for one's own peace.

2. **Fear of Vulnerability**: Forgiveness can make individuals feel exposed. This fear can prevent them from taking the necessary steps toward healing, as they worry about being hurt again or feel unworthy of reconciliation.
3. **Desire for Justice**: When wronged, the instinctual response may be a desire for justice. This desire can hinder the forgiveness process; realizing that forgiveness does not negate the need for accountability can help shift this mindset.
4. **Unrealistic Expectations**: Some may enter the forgiveness process with unrealistic expectations—believing that it will instantly resolve all feelings of hurt. Understanding that forgiveness is a journey can help manage these expectations.
5. **Lack of Understanding**: Misconceptions about forgiveness can create barriers. Educating oneself about its true nature can facilitate a smoother path to healing.
6. **Fear of Losing Identity**: For some, holding onto past grievances becomes part of their identity. Recognizing that forgiveness allows for personal growth can help in this regard.
7. **Timing**: Forgiveness is not a linear process. It's important to allow oneself the time to process emotions before attempting to forgive.

8. **Inability to Communicate**: Some may want to forgive but feel unable to express their feelings. Exploring alternative communication methods, such as writing a letter, can provide an outlet.

In conclusion, while the path to forgiveness can be fraught with challenges, recognizing and addressing these obstacles can pave the way for healing. Approaching forgiveness with understanding and compassion—both for oneself and for others—can create a foundation for deeper connections and a more fulfilling future.

Understanding the Power of Forgiveness

Forgiveness is not about excusing or condoning harmful behavior. Instead, it is about releasing the burden of resentment and reclaiming your peace. Here are some insights into the power of forgiveness:

- **Liberates You**: By forgiving, you free yourself from the emotional weight of anger and bitterness, allowing space for healing and growth.
- **Restores Relationships**: Forgiveness can mend broken bonds and open the door to renewed understanding and connection.
- **Fosters Empathy**: It encourages you to see situations from different perspectives, cultivating compassion.

Steps to Forgiveness

Forgiving someone can be a challenging process, but it is a

HEALING RELATIONSHIPS THROUGH FORGIVENESS

journey worth undertaking. Here are steps to guide you:

1. **Acknowledge the Pain**: Recognize the hurt and allow yourself to feel your emotions without judgment.
2. **Reflect on the Experience**: Consider the situation and what you can learn from it. Understanding the root causes can provide clarity.
3. **Let Go of Resentment**: Release the hold resentment has on you. Visualize letting go of negative emotions.
4. **Extend Forgiveness**: Offer forgiveness to the person, even if they haven't apologized. This act is for your healing.
5. **Seek Closure**: If possible, communicate your forgiveness to the person. If not, write a letter expressing your feelings and intentions, even if you don't send it.

Embracing the Journey of Healing

Embracing the journey of healing through forgiveness is an act of courage that not only nurtures your relationships but also mends your own spirit. As you navigate this path, remind yourself that forgiveness is a profound gift you offer to yourself. It is a source of inner peace and a catalyst for deeper connections with others. By letting go of past grievances, you free your heart to love more fully and live more authentically. Embrace this journey, for in forgiving, you illuminate your own path toward joy and resilience.

CHAPTER 21
Mindset and Personal Growth

"Success is not final, failure is not fatal: It is the courage to continue that counts." — Winston Churchill

As we journey through life, we encounter challenges that can either hinder our progress or propel us toward growth. The difference often lies in our mindset. Embracing a growth mindset allows us to see challenges as opportunities for learning and self-improvement.

A growth mindset, as coined by psychologist Carol Dweck, is the belief that our abilities and intelligence can be developed through dedication and hard work. This perspective fosters resilience, which is essential for anyone seeking personal growth. When we adopt a growth mindset, we begin to view setbacks not as failures but as valuable lessons guiding us toward our goals.

Transforming Challenges into Opportunities

Those with a growth mindset are more likely to respond constructively when faced with adversity. Instead of succumbing to feelings of inadequacy, they analyze the situation, reflect on what can be learned, and apply those insights to future endeavors.

Strategies for Cultivating a Growth Mindset

1. **Embrace Challenges**: Seek out situations that push your boundaries. Actively pursuing challenging experiences builds resilience.
2. **Learn from Criticism**: View feedback as a valuable opportunity for growth.
3. **Celebrate Effort, Not Just Results**: Shift focus from achieving outcomes to valuing the effort and learning process.
4. **Cultivate Curiosity**: Foster a desire to learn by exploring new subjects and engaging with diverse individuals.
5. **Reflect Regularly**: Journaling can be a powerful tool for tracking your growth.
6. **Surround Yourself with Growth-Oriented Individuals**: Engage with people who embrace a growth mindset.

Reflection Question

Think about a current challenge in your life. How can you shift your perspective to see it as an opportunity for growth?

What lesson could you learn from this experience that will bring you closer to your goals?

CHAPTER 22
Maintaining Your Radiance

"Your energy introduces you before you even speak." — Claritza Rausch Peralta

As you continue on your path of personal growth and empowerment, sustaining your radiance becomes vital. This is not merely a destination but an ongoing journey that requires consistent effort and care. In this chapter, we will delve into daily practices and strategies that empower you to nurture your mind, body, and spirit, ensuring that your inner light continues to shine brightly through every challenge and triumph you encounter.

Daily Practices for Radiance

To keep your radiance alive, engage in daily practices that nurture your mind, body, and spirit.

1. **Mindfulness and Meditation**: Set aside time each day for mindfulness or prayer.
2. **Physical Activity**: Engage in regular physical activity that you enjoy.
3. **Positive Affirmations**: Begin each day with affirmations that reinforce your worth and potential.
4. **Journaling**: Use journaling as a tool for self-reflection and growth.
5. **Gratitude Practice**: Cultivate gratitude by acknowledging the blessings in your life.

Embracing Change and Growth

- **Adaptability**: Be open to new experiences and willing to adapt.
- **Lifelong Learning**: Seek opportunities for personal and professional growth.
- **Self-Compassion**: Treat yourself with kindness and understanding.
- **Goal Reassessment**: Regularly assess and adjust your goals to align with your evolving values.

As you continue your journey, remember that maintaining your radiance is an ongoing commitment to yourself. It's about embracing change, learning continuously, and growing through every experience. Each step you take, no matter how small, nurtures the light within you, allowing it to shine even brighter.

Today, take one intentional step toward sustaining your

MAINTAINING YOUR RADIANCE

radiance. Whether it's through a moment of mindfulness, a conversation with a loved one, or an act of kindness toward yourself, let this action be a testament to your commitment to living vibrantly.

Remember, your radiance is not something to be attained—it's something to be sustained. Your journey is uniquely yours, filled with opportunities to illuminate the path not only for yourself but for those around you. So, shine brightly every day, knowing that your energy creates the world around you.

Affirmation: *"I am a radiant being, filled with light and love. I nurture my radiance daily, creating a life of joy, purpose, and connection."*

Carry this affirmation with you as a reminder of your power and potential. Let it inspire you to take the next step, knowing that each moment of radiance enhances your life and the lives of those you touch. You are the light the world needs—shine on.

CHAPTER 23
Sharing Your Radiance

"A candle loses nothing by lighting another candle." — James Keller

Living a radiant life is not just about personal fulfillment; it is also about inspiring and uplifting those around you. In this final chapter, we explore how you can share your radiance with the world and make a positive impact.

Ways to Share Your Light

1. **Acts of Kindness**: Perform acts of kindness to create a ripple effect of positivity.
2. **Mentorship**: Offer guidance and support to those on their journeys.
3. **Community Involvement**: Engage in community activities that align with your values.

4. **Storytelling**: Share your story authentically to motivate and connect with others.

Building a Legacy of Radiance

As you continue to live radiantly, consider the legacy you wish to leave behind. By living authentically and sharing your light, you create a lasting legacy of empowerment and positivity.

Bonus Chapter: Navigating Life's Transitions

"For I know the plans I have for you, declares the Lord, plans for welfare and not for evil, to give you a future and a hope." — Jeremiah 29:11 (ESV)

Transitions are an inevitable aspect of life. Whether you're relocating to a new city, embarking on a fresh career path, or navigating changes in personal relationships, these moments often stir a blend of excitement and anxiety. In this bonus chapter, we will delve into the emotional landscape of life's transitions, providing you with the tools to navigate these significant changes with grace, trust, and resilience. Embrace the journey, for within these transitions lie opportunities for profound transformation.

Understanding Transitions

Transitions often bring about a whirlwind of emotions. It's essential to recognize that feeling a range of emotions is entirely natural during these times. Understanding this can help you approach changes with a more balanced perspective. Remember, God is with you in these moments, guiding your steps and providing comfort. Leaning into your faith can serve as a source of strength and clarity.

The Three Stages of Transition

1. Endings: Every transition begins with an ending. It's important to acknowledge and honor what you are leaving behind. Reflect on the experiences and relationships that have shaped you, and trust that God has a purpose for the journey that lies ahead.
2. The Neutral Zone: This is the in-between phase where uncertainty often reigns. During this time, seek God's wisdom through prayer. Allow His presence to provide peace amidst the chaos. Embrace this period as a time for reflection and growth, understanding that it is a necessary step in your transition.
3. New Beginnings: As you step into new opportunities, embrace them with an open heart. Remember that God is orchestrating these new paths for your growth and development. Approach these beginnings with hope and excitement, knowing that each new chapter is filled with potential.

Embracing Change with Gratitude

Practicing gratitude can significantly shift our perspective during periods of change. By focusing on what we have rather than what we fear losing, we can cultivate a more positive outlook. Take time to reflect on the blessings in your life and the lessons learned from past experiences. Developing a heart full of gratitude reveals God's grace in every transition and guides you toward a hopeful future.

Allow God to Write Your Story

I recently listened to an inspiring message by Joel Osteen that emphasized the power of self-improvement. It reminded me that God can transform our most broken narratives into the most beautiful stories. Sometimes, we must release our desire to control every aspect of our lives and allow God to write our story.

No matter the challenges we face, remember that God tests us to refine our character. In our commitment to personal growth, let's not forget that true radiance comes from within. Embrace the journey, trust in His plans, and know that every transition is an opportunity for transformation.

Conclusion

As you close the pages of *The Radiance Within: Reclaim Your Power, Rewrite Your Story*, I hope you feel a renewed sense of purpose, clarity, and empowerment. This journey you've embarked upon is just the beginning of a lifelong adventure toward authenticity and joy. Remember, the radiance you seek is already within you, waiting to be nurtured and shared with the world.

Throughout this book, you've explored the depths of self-discovery, resilience, and personal growth. You've learned to break through limiting beliefs, embrace vulnerability, and foster meaningful connections. These insights and tools are now yours to wield, guiding you as you navigate your unique path.

I encourage you to take a meaningful step that resonates with the insights you've gained. Whether it's establishing a new boundary, crafting a vision board, or reaching out to someone who inspires you, approach this action with intention and bravery. Here are some ideas to help you begin:

- **Craft a Vision Board**: Set aside time to visualize your dreams and aspirations.
- **Start a Gratitude Journal**: Jot down three things you're grateful for each day.
- **Establish a New Goal**: Identify a goal that aligns with your core values.
- **Reach Out to Someone**: Connect with an inspiring individual or someone you can support.
- **Adopt a Self-Care Routine**: Allocate time each day to care for your mind, body, and spirit.

Additionally, consider diving into *The Radiance Within: A 12-Week Personal Development Workbook*. This workbook provides structured guidance to further enhance your personal growth. By committing to this action, you honor yourself and set off a ripple effect that can inspire those around you.

CONCLUSION

Final Note from the Author

As I reflect on the journey we've embarked upon together through these pages, my heart overflows with gratitude. Writing *The Radiance Within* has been a labor of love—a heartfelt endeavor to share my experiences, struggles, and growth with you. More than anything, it has been my way of reminding you that no matter where you've been, you are never alone.

In each chapter, I hoped to offer not just words but a beacon—a guiding light to reconnect you with the incredible power, strength, and beauty that reside within you. Life brings challenges, and I understand feelings of doubt and uncertainty. Yet, I also know the transformative power of choosing ourselves, the courage to let go, and the resilience to rise stronger than before. This journey may not be easy, but it is profoundly worthwhile.

I hope you feel inspired to embrace your radiance, stand tall in your worth, and move forward with unwavering courage. You deserve a life that reflects the fullness of who you are. You deserve a life that shines brightly.

Take the wisdom you've gained here, nurture it, and allow it to flourish. And always remember: you are radiant, powerful, and capable of rewriting your story in ways you might not yet envision. Hold this truth close to your heart and carry it with you every step of the way.

As we part ways, let us take a moment to pause in gratitude and hope:

May we find strength in our struggles and light in our

darkness. May we embrace the love that surrounds us and carry it forward into the world. May our journeys be filled with courage, compassion, and the radiant joy that comes from within.

The Radiance Within: Chapter Notes

Part 1: The Foundation of Radiance

CHAPTER 1: BREAKING THROUGH THE DARKNESS

- **Key Themes:** Resilience, self-discovery, and embracing vulnerability.
- **Takeaway:** Our journey through darkness reveals inner strength. Facing challenges head-on leads to personal growth.
- **Example:** Personal story of uncovering family secrets and finding strength in adversity.

CHAPTER 2: DEFINING YOUR TRUE SELF

- **Key Themes:** Authenticity, self-love, and redefining inner voice.
- **Takeaway:** Listening to your true self involves shedding societal expectations and embracing your authentic identity.
- **Example:** Journaling and introspection inspired by Elizabeth Gilbert and J.K. Rowling.

CHAPTER 3: CULTIVATING SELF-AWARENESS

- **Key Themes:** Mindfulness, introspection, and emotional intelligence.
- **Takeaway:** Self-awareness is crucial for personal growth and involves understanding emotions, thoughts, and actions.
- **Example:** Mindfulness exercises and journaling for introspection.

CHAPTER 4: BLOSSOMING THROUGH FAITH AND ACTION

- **Key Themes:** Faith, intuition, and purposeful action.

- **Takeaway:** Faith combined with decisive action leads to personal transformation and the fulfillment of dreams.
- **Example:** Inspirational figures like Oprah Winfrey and Steve Harvey.

CHAPTER 5: RECLAIMING YOUR POWER

- **Key Themes:** Self-love, boundaries, and empowerment.
- **Takeaway:** Reclaiming your power involves setting boundaries and putting yourself first.
- **Example:** Personal journey of walking away from toxic relationships.

PART 2: EMBRACING RADIANCE

CHAPTER 6: HEALING THE WOUNDS

- **Key Themes:** Grief, healing, and resilience.
- **Takeaway:** Healing involves acknowledging pain, finding purpose in it, and transforming it into strength.
- **Example:** Personal healing journey after losing a loved one.

CHAPTER 7: SELF-CARE AS EMPOWERMENT

- **Key Themes:** Self-care, well-being, and empowerment.
- **Takeaway:** Self-care is essential for empowerment and involves nurturing mind, body, and spirit.
- **Example:** 30-day self-care challenge focusing on mindfulness, nutrition, rest, and joy.

CHAPTER 8: DEVELOPING EMOTIONAL INTELLIGENCE

- **Key Themes:** Self-regulation, empathy, and social skills.
- **Takeaway:** Emotional intelligence enhances relationships and involves managing emotions and understanding others.
- **Example:** Practical strategies for improving emotional intelligence.

CHAPTER 9: VISIONING YOUR WAY TO SUCCESS

- **Key Themes:** Visualization, dreams, and goal-setting.
- **Takeaway:** Visualization transforms dreams into reality by creating a clear vision and engaging emotions.

- **Example:** Vision board creation inspired by Terri Savelle Foy, Oprah Winfrey, and Jim Carrey.

Part 3: Creating Your Dream Life

CHAPTER 10: GOAL SETTING WITH HEART AND PURPOSE

- **Key Themes:** Goal-setting, alignment, and purpose.
- **Takeaway:** Setting goals aligned with personal values ensures fulfillment and motivation.
- **Example:** Structured approach to breaking down long-term goals into actionable steps.

CHAPTER 11: OVERCOMING FEAR AND BUILDING RESILIENCE

- **Key Themes:** Fear, resilience, and personal growth.
- **Takeaway:** Overcoming fear requires acknowledging it and building resilience through a growth mindset.
- **Example:** Techniques for reframing fear and fostering resilience.

CHAPTER 12: MANIFESTATION IN ACTION

- **Key Themes:** Manifestation, faith, and inspired action.

- **Takeaway:** Manifestation involves aligning actions with intentions and trusting the process.
- **Example:** The journey of manifestation and the power of affirmations.

PART 4: EMPOWERING OTHERS THROUGH RADIANCE

CHAPTER 13: BREAKING FREE FROM LIMITING BELIEFS

- **Key Themes:** Limiting beliefs, empowerment, and transformation.
- **Takeaway:** Identifying and reframing limiting beliefs leads to personal liberation and empowerment.
- **Example:** Exercises for challenging and replacing limiting beliefs.

CHAPTER 14: THE POWER OF RENEWAL

- **Key Themes:** Renewal, reinvention, and embracing change.
- **Takeaway:** Renewal involves letting go of the old to embrace new growth opportunities.
- **Example:** Reflective exercise for spring cleaning your life.

THE RADIANCE WITHIN: CHAPTER NOTES

CHAPTER 15: THE ART OF LEADERSHIP AND INFLUENCE

- **Key Themes:** Leadership, empathy, and motivation.
- **Takeaway:** Effective leadership requires empathy, integrity, and a compelling vision.
- **Example:** Strategies for leading by example and fostering collaboration.

CHAPTER 16: INSPIRING OTHERS THROUGH YOUR STORY

- **Key Themes:** Authenticity, inspiration, and support.
- **Takeaway:** Sharing your story inspires others and fosters a community of support and growth.
- **Example:** Encouragement to become a source of inspiration for others.

CHAPTER 17: BUILDING TRUST AND EFFECTIVE COMMUNICATION

- **Key Themes:** Trust, communication, and relationships.
- **Takeaway:** Building trust and effective communication strengthens relationships.
- **Example:** Techniques for fostering open dialogue and resolving conflicts.

CHAPTER 18: THE RADIANCE WITHIN

- **Key Themes:** Radiance, authenticity, and potential.
- **Takeaway:** Embracing your true self and recognizing your radiance leads to a fulfilling life.
- **Example:** Reflective exercise and letter to your future self.

PART 5: NURTURING RADIANCE IN RELATIONSHIPS

CHAPTER 19: BUILDING RADIANT CONNECTIONS

- **Key Themes:** Connections, support, and community.
- **Takeaway:** Meaningful relationships enhance our journey to radiance.
- **Example:** Steps for cultivating relationships and building a supportive community.

CHAPTER 20: HEALING RELATIONSHIPS THROUGH FORGIVENESS

- **Key Themes:** Forgiveness, healing, and empathy.
- **Takeaway:** Forgiveness releases resentment and fosters deeper connections.
- **Example:** Steps to guide the process of forgiveness.

THE RADIANCE WITHIN: CHAPTER NOTES

CHAPTER 21: MINDSET AND PERSONAL GROWTH

- **Key Themes:** Growth mindset, challenges, and self-improvement.
- **Takeaway:** A growth mindset transforms challenges into opportunities for learning.
- **Example:** Strategies for cultivating a growth mindset.

CHAPTER 22: MAINTAINING YOUR RADIANCE

- **Key Themes:** Sustaining radiance, self-care, and change.
- **Takeaway:** Daily practices and adaptability are key to maintaining radiance.
- **Example:** Embracing lifelong learning and self-compassion.

CHAPTER 23: SHARING YOUR RADIANCE

- **Key Themes:** Impact, positivity, and legacy.
- **Takeaway:** Sharing your radiance inspires others and creates a lasting impact.
- **Example:** Ways to share your light and build a legacy of empowerment.

About the Author

Claritza Rausch Peralta is a devoted mother, accomplished banking specialist, author, mentor, and entrepreneur. Having faced and overcome her own struggles, she now dedicates her work to empowering women to embrace their potential, find their inner strength, and rewrite their stories with purpose and faith. In her memoir, *Blossoming into Radiance*, she shares her journey of self-discovery and transformation, inspiring others to pursue personal growth and confidence.

Through her company, Radiant Dreams Co., Claritza provides valuable resources, mentorship, and guidance to foster healing, empowerment, and success. Her mission is to help women step into their true radiance and build lives filled with purpose and fulfillment.

To connect with Claritza and become part of a supportive community dedicated to personal development, visit www.radiantdreamsco.com. Join the journey and discover the transformative power of living radiantly.

www.ingramcontent.com/pod-product-compliance
Lightning Source LLC
LaVergne TN
LVHW051035070526
838201LV00009B/209